A/60/117/Rev.1
ST/ESA/299

DEPARTMENT OF ECONOMIC AND SOCIAL AFFAIRS

The Inequality Predicament

Report on the World Social Situation 2005

UNITED NATIONS
New York, 2005

DESA

The Department of Economic and Social Affairs of the United Nations Secretariat is a vital interface between global policies in the economic, social and environmental spheres and national action. The Department works in three main interlinked areas: (i) it compiles, generates and analyses a wide range of economic, social and environmental data and information on which States Members of the United Nations draw to review common problems and to take stock of policy options; (ii) it facilitates the negotiations of Member States in many intergovernmental bodies on joint course of action to address ongoing or emerging global challenges; and (iii) it advises interested Governments on the ways and means of translating policy frameworks developed in United Nations conferences and summits into programmes at the country level and, through technical assistance, helps build national capacities

Note

The designations employed and the presentation of the material in this publication do not imply the expression of any opinion whatsoever on the part of the Secretariat of the United Nations concerning the legal status of any country or territory or of its authorities, or concerning the delimitations of its frontiers.

The term "country" as used in the text of the present report also refers, as appropriate, to territories or areas.

The designations of country groups in the text and the tables are intended solely for statistical or analytical convenience and do not necessarily express a judgement about the stage reached by a particular country or area in the development process.

Mention of the names of firms and commercial products does not imply the endorsement of the United Nations.

Symbols of United Nations documents are composed of capital letters combined with figures.

A/60/117/Rev.1
ST/ESA/299
United Nations publication
Sales No. E.05.IV.5
ISBN 92-1-130243-9

Printed by the United Nations, New York

Preface

Since the series was launched in 1952, the *Report on the World Social Situation* has served as a foundation for discussions and policy analysis of socio-economic issues at the intergovernmental level. It has served to identify emerging social trends of international concern and analyze relationships among major development issues with national, regional and international dimensions.

The *2005 Report* continues that tradition by addressing the subject of inequality. In particular, it focuses on some of the growing inequalities that make it challenging, but all the more imperative, to reach the Millennium Development Goals. It shows us that we cannot advance the development agenda without addressing the challenges of inequality within and between countries—the widening gap between skilled and unskilled workers, the chasm between the formal and informal economies, the growing disparities in health, education and opportunities for social and political participation.

The *Report* identifies four areas of particular importance: addressing worldwide asymmetries resulting from globalization; incorporating explicitly the goal of reducing inequality in policies and programmes designed to achieve poverty reduction; expanding opportunities for employment, with particular attention to improving conditions in the informal economy; and promoting social integration and cohesion as key to development, peace and security.

By detailing some of the most critical issues affecting social development today, the *Report* can help guide decisive action to build a more secure and prosperous world in which people are better able to enjoy their fundamental human rights and freedoms. Overcoming the inequality predicament is an essential element of this quest.

KOFI A. ANNAN
Secretary-General

Contents

Figures

Tables

Explanatory notes

The following symbols have been used in tables throughout the *Report*:

Two dots (..) indicate that data are not available or are not separately reported.

A dash (—) indicates that the item is nil or negligible.

A hyphen (-) indicates that the item is not applicable.

A minus sign (–) indicates a deficit or decrease, except as indicated.

A full stop (.) is used to indicate decimals.

A slash (/) between years indicates a statistical year, for example, 1990/91.

Use of a hyphen (-) between years, for example, 1990-1991, signifies the full period involved, including the beginning and end years.

Annual rates of growth or change, unless otherwise stated, refer to annual compound rates.

Details and percentages in tables do not necessarily add to totals, because of rounding.

The following abbreviations have been used:

AIDS	acquired immunodeficiency syndrome
CIS	Commonwealth of Independent States
DAC	Development Assistance Committee
DHS	Demographic and Health Survey(s)
ECLAC	Economic Commission for Latin America and the Caribbean
ESAF	Enhanced Structural Adjustment Facility
EU	European Union
FAO	Food and Agriculture Organization of the United Nations
FDI	foreign direct investment
GATT	General Agreement on Tariffs and Trade
GDP	gross domestic product
GNI	gross national income
GNP	gross national product
G-7	Group of Seven major industrialized countries
HIV	human immunodeficiency virus
IFF	International Finance Facility
ILO	International Labour Organization
IMF	International Monetary Fund
NGO	non-governmental organization
ODA	official development assistance
OECD	Organisation for Economic Cooperation and Development
PRGF	Poverty Reduction and Growth Facility
PRSP	Poverty Reduction Strategy Paper
SDR	special drawing rights

TB	tuberculosis
TRIPS	Agreement on Trade-Related Aspects of Intellectual Property Rights
UNCTAD	United Nations Conference on Trade and Development
UNICEF	United Nations Children's Fund
VAT	value added tax
WHO	World Health Organization
WIDER	World Institute for Development Economics Research
WIID	World Income Inequality Database
WTO	World Trade Organization

Reference to dollars ($) indicates United States dollars, unless otherwise stated.

When a print edition of a source exists, the print version is the authoritative one. United Nations documents reproduced online are deemed official only as they appear in the United Nations Official Document System. United Nations documentation obtained from other United Nations and non-United Nations sources is for informational purposes only. The Organization does not make any warranties or representations as to the accuracy or completeness of such materials.

Unless otherwise indicated, the following country groupings and subgroupings have been used in the *Report*:

Developed market economies:

North America (excluding Mexico), Southern and Western Europe (excluding Cyprus, Malta, and Serbia and Montenegro), Australia, Japan, and New Zealand.

Economies in transition:

Albania, Bulgaria, Czech Republic, Hungary, Poland, Romania, Slovakia, and the former Union of Soviet Socialist Republics, comprising the Baltic Republics and the member countries of the Commonwealth of Independent States.

Developing countries (49 countries):

All countries in Africa, Asia and the Pacific (excluding Australia, Japan and New Zealand), Latin America and the Caribbean, Cyprus, Malta, and Serbia and Montenegro.

Where data are from UNESCO, the following regional groupings have been used:

Arab States and North Africa: Algeria, Bahrain, Djibouti, Egypt, Iraq, Jordan, Kuwait, Lebanon, Libyan Arab Jamahiriya, Mauritania, Morocco, Oman, Occupied Palestinian Territory, Qatar, Saudi Arabia, Sudan, Syrian Arab Republic, Tunisia, United Arab Emirates, and Yemen.

Central Asia: Armenia, Azerbaijan, Georgia, Kazakhstan, Kyrgyzstan, Mongolia, Tajikistan, Turkmenistan, and Uzbekistan.

Central and Eastern Europe: Albania, Belarus, Bosnia and Herzegovina, Bulgaria, Czech Republic, Croatia, Estonia, Hungary, Latvia, Lithuania, Poland, Republic of Moldova, Romania, Russian Federation, Serbia and Montenegro, Slovakia, Slovenia, the former Yugoslav Republic of Macedonia, Turkey, and Ukraine.

East Asia and the Pacific: Australia, Cambodia, China, Cook Islands, Democratic People's Republic of Korea, Fiji, Indonesia, Japan, Kiribati, Lao People's Democratic Republic, Malaysia, Marshall Islands, Myanmar, Nauru, Niue, New Zealand, Papua New Guinea, Philippines, Republic of Korea, Samoa, Solomon Islands, Thailand, Tonga, Tuvalu, Vanuatu, and Viet Nam.

Latin America and the Caribbean: Anguilla, Antigua and Barbuda, Aruba, Argentina, Bahamas, Barbados, Belize, Bermuda, Bolivia, Brazil, British Virgin Islands, Cayman Islands, Chile, Colombia, Costa Rica, Cuba, Dominica, Dominican Republic, Ecuador, El Salvador, Grenada, Guatemala, Guyana, Haiti, Honduras, Jamaica, Mexico, Montserrat, Netherlands Antilles, Nicaragua, Panama, Paraguay, Peru, Saint Kitts and Nevis, Saint Lucia, Saint Vincent and the Grenadines, Suriname, Trinidad and Tobago, Turks and Caicos Islands, Uruguay, and Venezuela.

North America and Western Europe: Andorra, Austria, Belgium, Canada, Cyprus, Denmark, Finland, France, Germany, Greece, Iceland, Ireland, Israel, Italy, Luxembourg, Malta, Monaco, Netherlands, Norway, Portugal, San Marino, Spain, Sweden, Switzerland, United Kingdom of Great Britain and Northern Ireland, and United States of America.

South and West Asia: Afghanistan, Bangladesh, Bhutan, India, Islamic Republic of Iran, Maldives, Nepal, Pakistan, and Sri Lanka.

Sub-Saharan Africa: Angola, Benin, Botswana, Burkina Faso, Burundi, Cameroon, Cape Verde, Central African Republic, Chad, Comoros, Congo, Côte d'Ivoire, Democratic Republic of the Congo, Equatorial Guinea, Eritrea, Ethiopia, Gabon, Gambia, Ghana, Guinea, Guinea-Bissau, Kenya, Lesotho, Liberia, Madagascar, Malawi, Mali, Mauritius, Mozambique, Namibia, Niger, Nigeria, Rwanda, Sao Tome and Principe, Senegal, Seychelles, Sierra Leone, Somalia, South Africa, Swaziland, Togo, Uganda, United Republic of Tanzania, Zambia, and Zimbabwe.

Least developed countries:

Afghanistan, Angola, Bangladesh, Benin, Bhutan, Burkina Faso, Burundi, Cambodia, Cape Verde, Central African Republic, Chad, Comoros, Democratic Republic of the Congo (formerly Zaire), Djibouti, Equatorial Guinea, Eritrea, Ethiopia, Gambia, Guinea, Guinea-Bissau, Haiti, Kiribati, Lao People's Democratic Republic, Lesotho, Liberia, Madagascar, Malawi, Maldives, Mali, Mauritania, Mozambique, Myanmar, Nepal, Niger, Rwanda, Samoa, Sao Tome and Principe, Senegal, Sierra Leone, Solomon Islands, Somalia, Sudan, Timor-Leste, Togo, Tuvalu, Uganda, United Republic of Tanzania, Vanuatu, Yemen, and Zambia.

Executive summary

The global commitment to overcoming inequality, or redressing the imbalance between the wealthy and the poor, as clearly outlined at the 1995 World Summit for Social Development in Copenhagen and endorsed in the United Nations Millennium Declaration, is fading. Eighty per cent of the world's gross domestic product belongs to the 1 billion people living in the developed world; the remaining 20 per cent is shared by the 5 billion people living in developing countries. Failure to address this inequality predicament will ensure that social justice and better living conditions for all people remain elusive, and that communities, countries and regions remain vulnerable to social, political and economic upheaval.

The present *Report on the World Social Situation* traces trends and patterns in economic and non-economic aspects of inequality and examines their causes and consequences. It focuses on the traditional aspects of inequality, such as the distribution of income and wealth, as well as inequalities in health, education, and opportunities for social and political participation. The *Report* also analyses the impact of structural adjustment, market reforms, globalization and privatization on economic and social indicators.

Ignoring inequality in the pursuit of development is perilous. Focusing exclusively on economic growth and income generation as a development strategy is ineffective, as it leads to the accumulation of wealth by a few and deepens the poverty of many; such an approach does not acknowledge the intergenerational transmission of poverty. A broader approach to poverty reduction includes social, economic and political dimensions, integrating improvements in health, education, economic development, and representation in legislative and judicial processes. It is the implementation of policies in these areas that contributes to the development of human capital, enabling the poor to realize their full productive potential. Addressing all aspects of poverty increases the odds that future generations will reap the benefits of today's policies rather than remaining trapped in a cycle of poverty.

Inequalities in income distribution and in access to productive resources, basic social services, opportunities, markets, and information can cause and exacerbate poverty. As emphasized in the recommendations of the World Summit for Social Development, it is crucial that policies and programmes for poverty reduction include socio-economic strategies to reduce inequality.

Addressing inequality requires efforts to achieve a balance between many complex, countervailing socio-economic forces. Although economic growth is necessary, it is not a sufficient condition to reduce poverty. Reforms are required in a number of different areas to increase the opportunities for and capabilities of the poor and other marginalized groups in order to spur inclusive growth and development and thereby reduce inequality.

A healthy, well-educated, adequately employed and socially protected citizenry contributes to social cohesion. Improved access by the poor to public assets and services (especially in the education and health sectors) and income transfer programmes to sustain the poorest families are essential to changing the structure of opportunities and are key to reducing the intergenerational transmission of poverty and inequality. Breaking the intergenerational poverty cycle is a vital component of an integrated and equitable poverty reduction strategy.

The World Summit for Social Development emphasized the need to ensure the provision of universal and equitable access to education and primary health care. Recognition of the importance of culture and tolerance, a people-centred approach to sustainable development, and the full development of human resources is also essential.

In spite of the compelling case for redressing inequality, economic and non-economic inequalities have actually increased in many parts of the world, and many forms of inequality have become more profound and complex in recent decades.

Income differentials have narrowed among the high-income countries that are not members of the Organisation for Economic Cooperation and Development, with the exception of a few countries that have pursued liberalization and deregulation policies; among most other countries income inequalities have worsened since the 1980s, and the income gap between high- and low-income countries has widened.

In many parts of the world persistently high levels of poverty are at least partly attributable to inadequate incomes. The proportion of the world's population living in extreme poverty declined from 40 to 21 per cent between 1981 and 2001. Nonetheless, many countries continue to experience high levels of poverty. China and India, which together account for close to 40 per cent of the global population, contribute greatly to the overall positive picture. Elsewhere, the levels and persistence of poverty are more pronounced.

The large and growing chasm between the formal and informal economies in many parts of the world strengthens the case for reducing inequality. Those who are part of the formal economy generally fall among the "haves" in society, as they are more likely to earn decent wages, receive job-related benefits, have secure employment contracts, and be covered by labour laws and regulations. In contrast, those in the informal economy are typically among the "have nots"; they are often excluded from various legal protections and are unable to access the basic benefits or enjoy the fundamental rights granted to those in the formal economy. Since most poor people work informally, the recent expansion of the informal economy in many countries has major implications for reducing poverty and inequality.

Access to jobs is essential for overcoming inequality and reducing poverty. People who cannot secure adequate employment are unable to generate an income sufficient to cover their health, education and other basic needs and those of their families, or to accumulate savings to protect their households from the vicissitudes of the economy. The unemployed are among the most vulnerable in society and are therefore prone to poverty.

The global employment situation is characterized by extreme inequality. Some 186 million people were unemployed in 2003, accounting for 6.2 per cent of the total working population, up from 140 million a decade earlier. Among developed countries unemployment has generally declined in recent years; however, much of the developing world has experienced high and even rising unemployment. This escalating unemployment within the latter group has several underlying causes, including high labour force growth rates and continued reliance on policies exclusively focused on macroeconomic stability.

Liberalization policies entail changes in labour laws and institutions and account for major changes in the labour market. The process of economic liberalization is typically marked by greater wage flexibility and the erosion of minimum wages, a reduction in public sector employment, declining employment protection, and the weakening of employment laws and regulations. The desire of developing countries to attract foreign investment and expand exports frequently leads to a "race to the bottom" with labour protection and environmental standards often ignored or compromized, ostensibly to make the countries more competitive in the international market. External competitive pressures therefore restrict the ability of developing countries to pursue key aspects of social policy.

In many countries, the failure to address the needs of poor people as part of a strategy for sustained growth has been a major obstacle to reducing poverty. High rates of fertility and population growth, large pools of unskilled labour, and the HIV/AIDS epidemic have also played a role in perpetuating poverty, especially in Africa. Internal and international migration are strongly linked to poverty as well; sending communities become poorer, as they tend to lose their most economically active members, and in receiving communities, migrants are likely to be poorly integrated and vulnerable to extreme poverty. The growing tendency for people to move in and out of poverty can mean that those who are not thought to be poor in a particular period may be overlooked by social assistance programmes. Deepening levels of rural poverty, along with the increasing urbanization of poverty, also pose new challenges to development.

Various non-economic inequalities also impinge on the progress of development in many countries. For example, though most countries have succeeded in expanding educational access in general, large disparities persist in access to both primary and higher-level education. Disparities in child health and mortality are pronounced and reflect underlying inequalities in access to quality care for mothers and their children. One area of concern is access to immunisation, which, despite significant increases in coverage in recent decades, remains highly differentiated by factors such as maternal education and place of residence. Malnutrition and hunger are at the root of global differentials in health and survival.

The HIV/AIDS epidemic has deepened both economic and non-economic inequalities. The situation is particularly alarming in sub-Saharan Africa, which has been hardest hit by the epidemic. The region is performing poorly with respect to both economic and non-economic indicators, and the gap between many countries in the region and the rest of the world is widening. Of special concern is the contribution of HIV/AIDS to the widening differentials in life expectancy across countries and world regions.

Gender dimensions are deeply embedded in observed inequalities. There are persistent gender gaps in access to education, decent employment, and fair and equal remuneration. In most countries, the increase in the numbers of women in the workforce over the past two decades masks the deterioration in the terms and conditions of employment, as women tend to secure jobs with lower pay. Women's poorer access to economic and non-economic opportunities is often at the root of their lower status in many societies; as a consequence, they may be subject to abuse and sexual exploitation and rendered voiceless in issues relating to their own welfare.

In the past decade, greater attention has been directed towards improving the status of various social groups, as demonstrated by the substantial efforts undertaken to ensure the rights of indigenous peoples and persons with disabilities and to address poverty among older persons and unemployment among youth. There appears to have been less of an interest in policies to equalize the distribution of income and wealth, however.

Providing social protection for the older members of society is especially important. Benefits for older persons often extend to the whole family, as the money and other resources they possess are invariably shared with their offspring and younger dependants, strengthening the family resource base and contributing to the welfare of current and future generations. Governments should therefore identify policy changes that may be needed to sustain and support older persons rather than looking for ways to cut costs.

Democracy and the rule of law are essential for the elimination of institutionalized inequalities that have prevented the successful integration of marginalized groups into society. Although the twentieth century saw a rise in the number of democratic governments globally, the pace and implementation of democratization have been uneven. The consolidation of democracy is a process, and it may take many years for the roots of democracy to take hold. During this transition it is necessary for a sovereign State, through its internal actions and institutions, to reinforce democratic principles by promoting human rights and encouraging the political participation of all groups. It is essential that democratic freedoms be enshrined in legislation and backed up by political will. Many policy prescriptions are designed without adequate analysis of how the poorest and most vulnerable (especially women) are likely to be affected; consequently, these groups remain marginalized in a number of countries. Achieving success and sustainability in the development process requires the engagement of all groups to ensure that the needs of all people are addressed, and ultimately to promote equality.

The recent explosive growth in international migration is a response to perceived inequalities of opportunity between sending and receiving countries. High migration streams engender and exacerbate inequalities. Many migrants encounter circumstances that leave them vulnerable to exploitation in their countries of destination. Inequalities between migrants and resident populations are even wider when migrants constitute a source of cheap labour. Migrant earnings account for a sizeable share of the increasing flows of remittances, especially to poor countries. These remittances constitute the second-largest source of financial flows into developing countries after foreign direct investment and have surpassed official development assistance (ODA) globally.

Conspicuously absent from the global development agenda are a number of issues of particular interest to developing countries, including international labour mobility, the facilitation of remittances, international taxation on financial flows, financing mechanisms to address the special needs of marginalized countries and social groups, and mechanisms to ensure macroeconomic policy coherence.

Asymmetric globalization is an important source of rising inequality. As rapid globalization is occurring in the economic realm, the international social agenda, for which there are very weak accountability and enforcement mechanisms, remains relatively marginalized. There is a compelling need to create the necessary space in the international system for the provision of political, social, economic and environmental "global public goods". Insufficient public oversight has hitherto contributed to a situation in which the costs and benefits of globalization are not equally shared among countries and peoples.

Even in settings in which institutions prove to be adequate, the shortage of financial resources can cripple social development efforts. There has been ample discussion of possible ways to finance social development, with many countries undertaking commitments to increase the amount and quality of ODA. High levels of military spending have impeded the progress of social development, as those countries that allocate a substantial share of total government expenditure to the defence sector also tend to reserve the lowest portion of the budget for the social sectors. Global insecurity resulting from the rise in international terrorism has contributed to increased national security spending in many countries, leading to a further diversion of resources from social development. The violence associated with national and international acts of terrorism should be viewed in the context of social inequality and disintegration. In situations in which inequalities are extreme and there is competition over scarce resources, the likelihood of social disintegration and violence increases. Violence is more common where inequalities are greater, and trends suggest that growing up in poverty often leads to social exclusion, which can contribute to crime. Countries with high rates of poverty and inequality generally have poorer social support and safety nets, more unequal access to education, and fewer opportunities for young people. The likelihood of armed conflict is also greater under such adverse social conditions.

The way forward: policies to reduce inequality

It is evident that inequalities jeopardize efforts to achieve social justice and development. The comprehensive vision of social development agreed upon at the World Summit for Social Development ought to dominate and shape the agendas of national Governments and international organizations so that the strategic benchmarks identified in the Millennium Development Goals and the larger objectives of sustainable and equitable social and economic development can be achieved.

To create the conditions necessary for social development, urgent attention is required in four areas of particular importance. First, worldwide asymmetries deriving from globalization need to be redressed. Second, the goal of reducing inequality must be explicitly incorporated in policies and programmes aimed at poverty reduction; in particular, specific measures should be included to guarantee access by marginalized groups to assets and opportunities. In this context, the Millennium Development Goals should not be seen as a substitute for the larger United Nations development agenda, which provides a much broader development framework. Third, priority must be given to expanding and improving opportunities for employment. It is essential that employment strategies not only address job creation but also promote decent working conditions in which equality, security and dignity figure prominently. Finally, social integration and cohesion must be promoted as key to development, peace and security. Social integration requires the full participation of all groups in the social, economic, political and cultural spheres. Groups that tend to be subject to discrimination, including indigenous peoples and persons with disabilities, require particular attention in policy-making and implementation.

The persistence, and even deepening, of various forms of inequality worldwide should not be accepted with equanimity. With the unprecedented wealth and resources, technical expertise, and scientific and medical knowledge available in the world today, the most vulnerable in society cannot continue to be left so far behind. Macroeconomic and trade liberalization policies, economic and financial globalization, and changes in labour market institutions cannot be disconnected from the struggle to achieve social development, equality and social justice. The failure to pursue a comprehensive, integrated approach to development will perpetuate the inequality predicament, for which everyone pays the price.

JOSÉ ANTONIO OCAMPO
Under-Secretary-General
Department of Economic and Social Affairs

Introduction

History is teeming with cautionary tales of the unintended consequences of narrow economic interests overriding the needs of the people and the issues that matter most. It is also full of seminal moments when a visionary course was charted and society moved forward. One such moment occurred 60 years ago with the founding of the United Nations. Not long after its establishment, its Member States charted a visionary course of action by recognizing that freedom, justice and peace in the world is based on recognition of the inherent dignity, equality and inalienable rights of all.[1]

The year 2005 marks the commemoration of other seminal moments, including the fifth anniversary of the Millennium Summit of the United Nations and the tenth anniversary of the World Summit for Social Development. Together, these unprecedented gatherings of heads of State and Government represent a resounding affirmation of the need "to promote social progress and better standards of life in larger freedom", as enshrined in the Charter of the United Nations.[2]

The timing of the World Summit for Social Development was significant. Public sentiment for the ideal of "equal opportunity for all" had been reawakened by the historic dismantling of apartheid, one of the most blatantly institutionalized forms of injustice and inequality ever in existence. The Summit was, above all, uniquely equipped to rally on behalf of those perennially at the bottom of the development ladder with a unified message that policies, in every realm and at all levels, must safeguard the standards of social justice. The convergence of these ideals characterized not only the end of a nationally systematized reign of oppression, but the beginning of a larger global struggle for social justice and equality.

This struggle, which has animated a great deal of debate and political action throughout the course of history, remains one of the dominant features of today's world. There has never been any illusion that inequality would be wholly and systematically eliminated, but the struggle to achieve even a measure of success has become increasingly difficult, as the global commitment to one of the most basic principles of equality—that there should be a better balance between the wealthiest and the poorest—appears to be fading.

It is profoundly disturbing that in a world in which unprecedented levels of wealth, technical expertise and scientific and medical knowledge have been attained, it is the most vulnerable in society that consistently lose ground during economic booms. One of the most visible by-products of globalization is access to new kinds of wealth and its propensity to increase inequality. Globalization has helped to accentuate trends that show the wealthiest 20 per cent of the planet accounting for 86 per cent of all private consumption and the poorest accounting for just above 1 per cent. Unless some headway is made in refocusing economic policies to help those left behind, progress towards poverty reduction remains uncertain.

The present *Report on the World Social Situation* traces the development and expansion of inequalities within and between countries, examining not only the distribution of income and wealth, but also opportunities, access, and political participation and influence, all of which have profound economic, social, political and cultural dimensions. It is argued in this *Report* that the rise in inequalities should not be considered in isolation or accepted with equanimity. The point is made that macroeconomic and trade liberalization policies, financial globalization and changes in labour market institutions cannot be disengaged from the struggle to achieve equality and social justice.

The trends highlighted in the *Report* demonstrate that rising inequalities are, at the most fundamental level, a clear and compelling manifestation of pervasive social injustice. Acknowledgment or recognition of such trends is not always coupled with coherent policies to halt or reverse them, however. Those following the current development discourse are well aware that there are deeply entrenched and strongly supported policies for economic growth that produce or exacerbate inequalities, and that efforts to protect poor people are routinely portrayed as increasing their burden on society.

As the *Report* illustrates, the global balance sheet on equality shows a critical deficit. One of the more ominous features of inequality is its intergenerational dimension, or the manner in which it is inherited by successive generations. Every society depends upon the transfer of knowledge and responsibility from one generation to another; however, inequality, poverty, unemployment and exclusion have the potential to alter or even arrest this natural course. Governments maintaining policies that sustain social fault lines run a substantial risk of exposing communities, countries and regions to various forms of social upheaval, potentially erasing the gains accruing from decades of social, economic and political investments.

Despite the fact that inequality exists in every realm and society, its mark is particularly disquieting in societies in which the political and economic institutions needed for long-term prosperity and stability are weak. Violence occurs more frequently in settings where there is an unequal distribution of scarce resources and power. The devastation wrought by such violence is deepened when societies turn a blind eye to atrocities such as genocide, slavery and the use of child soldiers in war. Similar to the legacy of apartheid, societies are likely to pay a heavy price for allowing poverty, unemployment and exclusion to continue to undermine the social fabric, contributing to persistent inequalities.

Notwithstanding the obstacles and setbacks, examples of recent efforts to attain equality are manifold. While some of the activity in this domain is directed towards equalizing wealth and income, much of it involves groups working to improve their status, win acceptance and secure the privileges and advantages enjoyed by other groups. This is perhaps most evident in the realm of gender. The women's movement has sought to give more than half of the world's population a voice. Women have traditionally had fewer opportunities than men and have faced greater obstacles, but many are now receiving some support in their struggle to achieve the goals their societies project.

Most workers are deeply entrenched in the informal economy; however, there is no galvanizing voice to speak for them. Informal workers generally have no benefits, social protection, or sense of security to bequeath to the next generation. Efforts to strengthen voting traditions, unions and lobbying efforts lack widespread political support. Like the poor and excluded, informal workers remain disenfranchised from the larger political movements in the struggle for equality and disconnected from participatory efforts to advance a more inclusive globalization. Informal workers are a constituency often mentioned but seldom heard; though they comprise a significant portion of today's global economy, they are, for the most part, scattered and marginalized.

For many countries national policy space is increasingly being reduced by liberalization policies that tend to accentuate asymmetric globalization and inequalities. The gradual diminution of openness in governance is hindering the average citizen's ability to establish a connection between public policy and situations of inequality. In such circumstances, when social inequalities and gaps in income and wealth reach levels that provoke unrest, it is unlikely that those policies contributing to inequality will receive the critical attention they deserve. Unfortunately, society accommodates itself to these new realities, creating a predicament whereby the obstacles to social justice are so overwhelming that those on the wrong side of the inequality equation simply despair and give up.

The world today is at a crossroads. If the vision of a shared future is to be carried forward, world leaders must seize every opportunity to take bold and decisive action to reverse negative trends. If humankind remains committed to fostering social integration and preventing the crystallisation of segmented societies, which would inevitably lead to more social conflict, they must aim higher than what merely appears achievable. The total development agenda of the United Nations should serve as a guide in such endeavours, with particular attention given to the decisions and recommendations emanating from the World Summit for Social Development.

The Reverend Martin Luther King, Jr., once issued the following appeal: "Through our scientific genius we have made of the world a neighbourhood; now through our moral and spiritual genius we must make of it a brotherhood."[3] It is clearly within the realm of human possibility to meet this challenge. Policies can and should redress trends that are neither morally acceptable nor politically or economically sound. A reshaping of priorities and attendant policies and strategies would provide not only the mechanisms for reducing inequalities but also the means to rectify injustices caused by short-sighted economic interests and political expediency. The evidence presented in this *Report* unflinchingly affirms the need to once again define the world in terms of its essential humanity and not solely in terms of its economic interests.

Notes

1 United Nations, Universal Declaration of Human Rights, General Assembly resolution 217 A (III) of 10 December 1948 (DPI/511).
2 Preamble to the Charter of the United Nations (1945).
3 Martin Luther King, Jr., "Facing the challenge of a new age", a speech presented in Montgomery, Alabama, on 3 December 1956.

Chapter I

The case for focusing on inequality

Can social development be achieved without focusing on inequality? If this question had been posed during the World Summit for Social Development,[1] the answer would have been a resounding "No!". A people-centred approach to development, as advocated in the Copenhagen Declaration on Social Development and the Programme of Action of the World Summit for Social Development, must have the principles of equity and equality at its core, as graphically illustrated in figure I.1, so that all individuals, regardless of their circumstances, have unimpeded access to resources and opportunities. The world today is far from equal, however, as evidenced by growing gaps between the rich and the poor. These gaps exist not only in income and assets, but also in the quality and accessibility of education, health care and employment opportunities, in the protection of human rights, and in access to political power and representation.

Through an analysis of the economic and socio-political dimensions of poverty and an examination of the impact of structural adjustment, market reform measures, targeting and privatization on access to education, health care and social protection programmes, this chapter builds a compelling case for redressing inequality in the pursuit of social development. The case for

Figure I.1. Policy framework: the three main pillars of social development centred on equity and equality

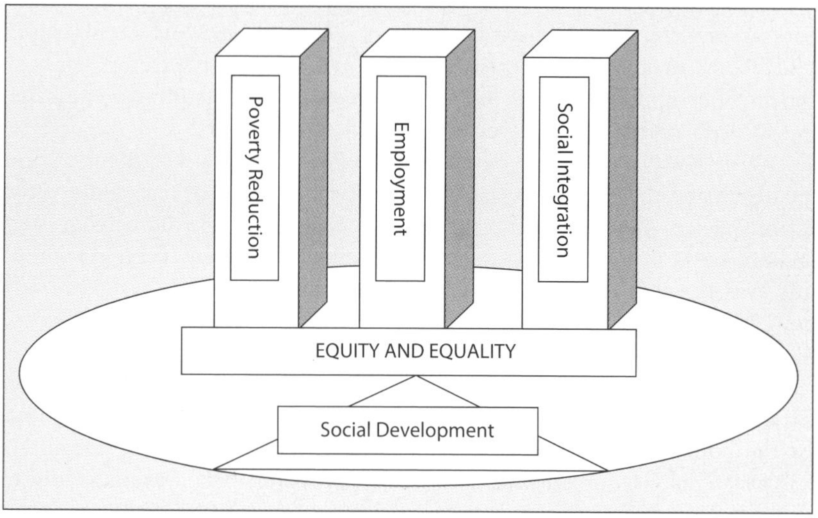

Poverty Reduction
Employment
Social Integration
EQUITY AND EQUALITY
Social Development

Source: Based on the concept of social development delineated at the World Summit for Social Development, held in Copenhagen from 6 to 12 March 1995.

focusing on inequality is further developed in chapter II, in which the divide between the formal and informal economies is spotlighted; the chapter highlights the disparities in wages, benefits, working conditions, tax burdens and legal protections, and how globalization and the drive for international competitiveness have served to widen the divide even further.

Linkages between poverty eradication and inequality

How relevant is inequality in the fight against poverty? To address this question, it is important to recognize the different forms poverty takes. While poverty has many dimensions, its two fundamental aspects are the lack of economic power owing to low incomes and assets, and the lack of socio-political power, as reflected in the limited access to social services, opportunities and information and often in the denial of human rights and the practice of discrimination. Without minimizing the importance of other dimensions of poverty, the present section focuses on these two critical aspects of poverty and their connection to inequality.

Inequality and the economic dimension of poverty

Poverty is typically defined in economic terms, as manifested in very low levels of income and consumption per capita or per household. In this context, conventional wisdom for a good portion of the past half-century has reflected the view that poverty is essentially a problem that can be fixed by raising incomes alone. The commitment to eradicating absolute poverty by halving the number of people living on less than US$ 1 per day, a Millennium Development Goal, is the most recent evidence of the income-focused view of poverty. The alternative concept of relative poverty, which highlights the inequalities in income distribution within and between societies, has been sidelined by undue emphasis on macroeconomic policies and market mechanisms dedicated to achieving rapid economic growth.

With the dissatisfaction over the outcomes of structural adjustment programmes and the over-reliance on market mechanisms that have led to a rise in inequality, the longstanding conviction that growth is the driving force behind poverty reduction is increasingly being questioned. There is mounting evidence that the impact of growth on poverty reduction is significantly lower when inequality is on the rise than when inequality is declining (Ravallion, 2004).

Furthermore, if growth contributes to increased inequality, then poverty may worsen—if not in absolute terms, then at least in relative terms, as the poor may find themselves comparatively worse off. For example, a low-wage policy coupled with tax incentives for large businesses may lead to rapid growth as investments increase; however, inequality is likely to worsen as lowered worker incomes adversely affect personal consumption and investments in human capital. Conversely, when the choice of growth strategy is consistent with the objective of reducing inequality, both absolute and relative poverty are apt to decline. Evidence from East Asia, for instance, indicates that a low level of income inequality is linked to fast growth, and policies to reduce poverty and income inequality that promote basic education and enhance labour demand further stimulate growth (Birdsall, Ross and Sabot, 1995).

Inequalities in land ownership also have a negative impact on growth and poverty reduction. Rural economies, in which land ownership is concentrated in the hands of a few while the majority remain landless, tend to face very high costs associated with labour shirking and supervision, inhibiting growth (Cornia and Court, 2001). Indeed, high inequality in the distribution of land has a significantly negative effect on future growth (Deininger and Squire, 1998).

High inequality in assets can also adversely affect growth, as it can limit progress in educational attainment and human capital accumulation—factors that contribute to higher productivity and ultimately to poverty reduction. Additionally, the social tensions caused by wide disparities in wealth and incomes can "erode the security of property rights, augment the threat of expropriation, drive away domestic and foreign investment and increase the cost of business security and contract enforcement" (Cornia and Court, 2001, p. 23).

It should be acknowledged, however, that equality can act as a disincentive to growth when productivity and creativity are not rewarded. At very low levels of inequality (as in socialist economies in the 1980s), "growth tends to suffer because the narrow range of wages does not sufficiently reward different capabilities and efforts, potentially leading to labour shirking and free-riding behaviour" (Cornia and Court, 2001, p. 23). Thus, it is useful to make a distinction between "constructive" inequality, which provides the incentive needed to move resources to where they will be used most efficiently; and "destructive" inequality, which generates envy and socially unproductive redistribution (Timmer and Timmer, 2004, p. 3). Finding the right balance between equality and competitiveness is essential.

Inequalities in access to production inputs and productive resources also have an impact on poverty reduction, as they raise the production and marketing costs of the poor, thereby rendering them less competitive and less able to raise their incomes. The poor have limited access to land, credit, information and markets. Since land is a key input to the production function of the rural poor, land ownership patterns and the displacement of the poor to less productive lands undermine their productive capacity. Access to credit and other financial services is crucial, as it allows the poor to establish their own small or micro enterprises. The recent success of microcredit programmes in helping the poor embark on new business ventures is evidence that providing more equal access to certain markets and services promotes poverty reduction. With the growth of the Internet and computer technologies, access to information and better communication is becoming much easier and increasingly important—not only for improving access to social services or enhancing the protection of rights, but also in allowing the poor to compete more fairly in the global market. Presently, the poor have unequal access to local and national markets for their outputs owing to the uneven dispersion of components of the transportation and communication infrastructure. Because the majority of the poor live in rural areas, policies that favour urban over rural areas worsen inequality and perpetuate poverty.

Inequality and the socio-political dimensions of poverty

A strictly economic approach to poverty reduction, which focuses solely on raising an individual's current income, does not translate into an intergenerational process of poverty reduction unless there is an accumulation of wealth or assets. A broader and more comprehensive approach to poverty reduction that also incorporates socio-political dimensions, including improvements in health and education and increased political representation in law-making, injects a dynamic, or intergenerational, view of poverty. This is so because investments in human capital enable the poor to realize their full productive potential over time. Addressing these other dimensions of poverty would not only improve the conditions of present generations, but would also increase the odds that future generations would continue to reap the benefits, thereby breaking the cycle of poverty. However, in spite of their centrality to poverty reduction, these socio-political dimensions are often downplayed or overlooked.

The goal of sustained poverty reduction cannot be achieved unless equality of opportunity and access to basic social services are ensured. Equality of opportunity means that all individuals have the same chance to participate in and contribute to the betterment of their own lives and the betterment of society: "Equitable access to resources is the key to equal opportunity, not only in the economic sense, but also in its social, cultural and political dimensions" (Ocampo, 2002b, p. 402). Expanding people's opportunities and capabilities will depend on the elimination of oppression and the provision of services and benefits such as basic education, health care and social safety nets (Sen, 1999).

Recent studies of inequality support the notion that inequality in access to basic public services contributes directly to poor health and deficiencies in the overall level of education. One such study of Latin America, for instance, reveals that despite high levels of public social spending, the poor are not benefiting because large segments of the low-income population are excluded from many areas of public welfare. The effects of entitlement restrictions in the region are reinforced by problems relating to access and quality in the provision of supposedly universal services (Lloyd-Sherlock, 2000). Similar empirical results show that in a number of African countries, spending on social services such as health care and education is not aptly directed to the poorest households (Castro-Leal and others, 1999; Sahn, Stifel and Younger, 1999; Sahn and Younger, 2000). Supporting these findings is evidence that the poor are typically subjected to the worst housing and living conditions, are disproportionately exposed to pollution and environmental degradation, and often find themselves in situations in which they are unable to protect themselves against violence and persecution. Taken together, these socio-political conditions create and sustain a vicious cycle of poverty and despair by contributing to the devaluation of human capital and potentially spawning additional problems that may have implications far into the future. They also have the effect of diminishing any gains achieved in income and poverty reduction.

In contrast to the foregoing, more equitable public sector investments have been found effective in improving access to education, health care and other social services. In Kerala, India, for example, it has been shown that high levels of education, especially among women, can short-circuit poverty, help reduce fertility rates and improve life expectancy. In Costa Rica, even though per capita gross national product (GNP) is one twelfth that in the United States, life expectancy is similar for the two countries, largely because of effective policies for basic education, communal health services and medical care (Sen, 1995).

Various studies have shown that public and private investment in human resources has helped mitigate poverty and inequality. In the Republic of Korea and Taiwan Province of China, government encouragement and support have been instrumental in the development of highly educated labour forces. The expansion of education has helped generate human resources with the technical and professional expertise needed for industrial upgrading and has enhanced opportunities for upward socio-economic mobility, including skill development and higher wages (Jomo, 2003). In Indonesia and Malaysia, reductions in inequality over an extended period can be attributed to government efforts aimed at redistribution and employment generation (Jomo, 2004). These are but a few of the country experiences that illustrate how redressing inequalities in access to basic social services, especially education, can lead to poverty reduction.

The poverty reduction equation is incomplete if inequality is not addressed from a political perspective as well, with particular attention given to issues such as discrimination and representation. As observed in a report of the United Nations Committee on Economic, Social and Cultural Rights, "Sometimes poverty arises when people have no access to existing resources because of who they are, what they believe or where they live. Discrimination may cause poverty, just as poverty may cause discrimination" (United Nations, 2001, para. 11).

Discrimination can take many forms, including the unequal enforcement of laws, even if the laws are fair. One of the most striking revelations in a recent study is "the extent to which the police and official justice systems side with the rich, persecute poor people and make poor people more insecure, fearful and poorer" (Narayan and others, 2000, p. 163). The selective application of laws translates into gender, racial and ethnic discrimination (forms of horizontal inequality) directed against the poorer segments of society. Typically compromised are labour and consumer laws that, for example, prohibit predatory pricing; the weak enforcement of such laws results in a "redistribution" from the poor to the rich. In other cases, the laws themselves may be inequitable. Land-grabbing, which displaces or uproots poor people and is typically the result of discrimination against this vulnerable group, can take the form of legalized expropriation.

Representation allows the poor to participate in decisions that affect their lives. Unequal representation is perhaps best illustrated by the contrast between the powerlessness of the poor and the dominance of the elite in the formulation of laws and regulations. Such a system often produces legal biases against the poor; laws governing land reform, property rights in general and intellectual property rights in particular are prone to this problem. Given the stakes involved, traditional elites are likely to resist active and informed participation by the poor in decision-making (United Nations, 2004a). More balanced representation is unlikely in the prevailing political environment, given the entrenched interests of those already in power and the fact that those most affected by income inequality often lack the capacity to influence economic, social and political decisions taken in their societies. The lack of an adequate income and the lack of representation reinforce each other in a vicious circle, since only by being able to participate in decision-making processes relating to laws and customs can the poor change the conditions that perpetuate their poverty.

As elucidated later in the *Report*, the increasing legitimization and institutionalization of civil society and the growing official recognition of the vital role civil society plays in the global development process have significantly improved the opportunities for marginalized groups to contribute to their own development. Nonetheless, the poor, minorities, indigenous peoples, rural residents, women and other groups with special needs frequently do not have much of a voice, even in issues that directly concern them. This situation exacerbates existing inequalities in access to infrastructure and services.

Even when the poor have some voice, the defence or protection of their rights entails certain costs, which can seriously drain their limited resources. This may be viewed as a "reverse incentive" that stands in direct contrast to the investment incentives granted to large business interests and corporations. Ultimately, when discrimination is high, the social and economic disincentives and penalties imposed on the poor are also high, further aggravating poverty.

In sum, inequalities in income distribution and representation and in access to productive resources, basic social services, opportunities, markets and information, together with discrimination, can exacerbate, if not cause, poverty. As affirmed in the recommendations of the World Summit for Social Development, it is crucial for poverty reduction policies and programmes to include socio-economic strategies with redistributive dimensions that will reduce inequality. Addressing inequality requires that a balance be achieved between many complex countervailing socio-economic forces that influence the level of inequality, the rate of economic growth and the impact of poverty reduction efforts. Although economic growth is necessary, relying on growth alone to reduce poverty is clearly insufficient; serious attention must also be directed to the many other factors contributing to inequality.

Structural reform, the public sector and inequality

Reducing inequality calls for reform measures to increase the opportunities and capabilities of the poor and other marginalized groups in order to spur inclusive growth and development. A healthy, well-educated, adequately employed and socially protected citizenry contributes to social cohesion. Thus, the redistributive potential of policies for health, education and social protection is of major significance. Improved access by the poor to public services and assets (especially in the health and education sectors) and income transfer programmes to sustain the poorest families are essential to changing the structure of opportunities and are key to reducing the intergenerational transmission of poverty and inequality. Breaking the intergenerational poverty cycle is a vital component of an integrated and equitable poverty reduction strategy.

Since the 1980s a number of Governments have undertaken measures to reduce spending on social services, increase cost efficiency, engage in privatization and target public services towards the poor. Some of the country members of the Organisation for Economic Cooperation and Development (OECD), for example, have pursued policies to reduce expenditures on universal social programmes such as unemployment compensation and old-age pensions, thereby reducing public transfers to low-income families (Weeks, 2004). In Latin America and the Caribbean, access to public services has been segmented; instead of benefiting the poorest, this move has actually worked against the objectives of equality (Economic Commission for Latin America and the Caribbean, 2000b).

Structural adjustment programmes were implemented in the 1980s and early 1990s with the expectation that economic growth rates for the countries undergoing structural adjustment would be higher and that once fiscal imbalances were addressed, the higher growth rates would be sufficient to generate social benefits. Actual experience proved otherwise, particularly in areas of sub-Saharan Africa and in many parts of Latin America and the Caribbean, with policy makers gradually realizing that pursuing economic stabilization policies at the expense of social policies produced negative long-term consequences.

The cumulative result of these structural reforms of the past two decades has been a rise in inequality in both developed and developing countries. In recognition of this negative impact, institutions such as the World Bank have begun to support social development as part of their overall poverty reduction strategies (see, for example, World Bank, 2004c). Clear evidence of this shift came in December 1999, when the boards of the World Bank and the International Monetary Fund (IMF) approved a new approach to the challenge of reducing poverty in low-income countries that essentially involved the development of country-owned strategies for tackling poverty, set out in national Poverty Reduction Strategy Papers (PRSPs). Tellingly, the name of the IMF country assistance programme was changed from Enhanced Structural Adjustment Facility (ESAF) to Poverty Reduction and Growth Facility (PRGF). By April 2005, a total of 45 countries had completed their first full PRSPs, and of those countries, 24 had finished preparing their first annual implementation progress reports; an additional 12 countries had completed their interim PRSPs (World Bank, 2005). The proliferation of these initiatives reflects the crucial role of social development in sustaining progress within the broader context of overall development.

The World Bank has recognized some of the multidimensional aspects of poverty, including exposure to vulnerability and risk, low levels of education and health, and powerlessness (World Bank, 2000). To these must be added the unequal distribution of assets such as land, capital, technology and education and unequal access to participation in policy-making. Although the PRSPs are much in line with the call by the World Summit for Social Development to include social development in structural adjustment programmes (United Nations, 1995), the Papers have yet to fully reflect the multifaceted character of poverty.

National efforts to remedy inequality spurred by structural reforms have included reshaping social security systems and the roles of key social sectors, with special emphasis placed on broadening coverage and improving benefits through more efficient management practices. Institutional changes have also been introduced with the aim of providing better services, improving targeting and linking resources to the quality of service.

Likewise, efforts are being made to reinforce the link between social programmes and the promotion of productive activities such as training. For example, some countries have shifted the focus of traditional welfare systems from entitlements to employment and human resources development for the most vulnerable groups. In addition, a number of Governments have undertaken social security reforms using targeting as a criteria for the provision of social services. These initiatives, in turn, have brought about changes in the patterns of resource allocation and intervention, the magnitude of social programmes and the administration of traditional safety nets (Morales-Gomez, 1999). Finally, the appropriate mix between the public and private sectors in the provision of public goods and equitable systems of regulation and subsidies is now reflected in the policy agenda in many countries.

Universal access to education, health care and social protection

Inequalities in educational access and outcomes, health status, employment opportunities, social protection, and other dimensions of social welfare are pervasive and growing in many countries. Education is typically viewed as a powerful factor in levelling the field of opportunity, as it provides individuals with the capacity to obtain a higher income and standard of living and enables those living in contaminated environments to overcome major health threats. By learning to read and write and acquiring technical or professional skills, people increase their chances of obtaining decent, better-paying jobs. Furthermore, there is considerable evidence that even in settings in which sanitation facilities are poor and piped water is unavailable, the children of educated mothers have much better prospects for survival than do the children of uneducated mothers. As these facts indicate, the importance of equal access to a well-functioning education system, particularly in relation to reducing inequalities, cannot be overemphasized.

Both within and between countries, wide differences in the quality and availability of education persist. Disparities in access to education are prevalent and tend to be determined by socio-economic and family background. Because such disparities are typically transmitted from generation to generation, access to educational and employment opportunities is to a certain degree inherited, with segments of the population systematically suffering exclusion.

Studies indicate that inequality declines as the average level of educational attainment increases, with secondary education producing the greatest payoff, especially for women (Cornia and Court, 2001). Recognizing these far-reaching implications, many countries in Asia and Latin America have assigned priority in their national agendas to ensuring universal access to and coverage of basic education, especially for girls, and to expanding secondary education (United Nations Educational, Scientific and Cultural Organization, 2005). Abolishing school fees and providing special incentives to encourage the most marginalized groups to attend school are also viewed as powerful tools for promoting educational equality. In countries in Africa and Latin America, cash and in-kind subsidies such as free school meals for poor households are being offered to promote school attendance (United Nations Millennium Project, 2005). Since improving equality is easier when educational resources are plentiful and growing, many countries have initiated changes in educational financing and resource allocation systems and are expanding the scope of private input (International Forum for Social Development, 2004).

Other educational reforms have focused on correcting deficiencies linked to the quality and relevance of what is taught in the classroom. Some of these reforms involve bringing qualitative changes in line with the evolving demands of the labour market. New technologies and increased competitiveness have placed greater demands on the labour force, making it imperative that a relevant basic education be universally accessible, and that scholastic content be adapted to ensure the acquisition of the skills needed in a changing knowledge-based economy. Knowledge and skills gaps have contributed to widening income disparities. Virtually without exception, wage differentials between skilled and unskilled labour, and particularly between university-educated workers and the rest of the labour force, have expanded (Ocampo, 2002b). In sum, greater attention must be given to ensuring universal access to a high-quality, relevant education and opportunities for training and skill development in order to reduce inequality and foster broader competitiveness in the labour market.

Health is another key input in the process of equitable development; health status not only affects the quality of life, but can also determine levels of opportunity and productivity. Patterns of inequality in health are characterized by the more disadvantaged segments of society being deprived of health-care services and excluded from the health-care system. Some of the recent reforms in the health sector have been aimed at ensuring universal access to primary health care, while others have focused on improving the quality of care and the efficiency with which health systems reach the poor and disadvantaged. Waiving health-care costs and fees for individuals who cannot afford to pay and providing direct conditional cash transfers to poor families to reward household behaviour such as bringing children to health centres for regular check-ups are some of the innovative, targeted approaches that have been adopted in a number of developing countries (World Health Organization, 2003).

Particular emphasis has been placed on improving child and maternal health outcomes in an effort to reduce the more than 10 million deaths among children and half a million deaths among mothers that occur annually (World Health Organization, 2005b). Initiatives often focus on improving the status of women in the community, encouraging disease prevention and teaching better parenting techniques. Central to these efforts is an integrated approach to family health care—one that begins with pregnancy and continues through childbirth and on into childhood. Both mothers and children benefit greatly from access to a continuum of care, in contrast to the fragmented and inconsistent care that typically prevails. Addressing child and maternal health issues is an effective way to alleviate the poverty that is both a cause and an effect of ill health.

Improved social protection mechanisms, including unemployment compensation, disability insurance, pensions, social security and other forms of income support, also constitute a fundamental component of strategies for reducing inequality and poverty. In the absence of adequate social protection, individuals and families, particularly those from the more vulnerable groups, are more likely to suffer serious hardship during periods of unemployment and transition. At present, social protection systems and institutions are weak and seriously underfunded in most countries, with almost 80 per cent of the world's population having little or no social protection coverage (Garcia and Gruat, 2003).

A common characteristic of social security schemes in Latin America is "segmented access", whereby coverage is provided for middle-income urban employees in the formal economy but rarely for the poor, who are also inadequately covered by welfare programmes (Economic Commission for Latin America and the Caribbean, 2000a). Likewise, some African countries have subsidy schemes for urban health facilities and universities that favour the rich at the expense of the poor (United Nations Development Programme, 1999). In developing countries undergoing macroeconomic reform, social protection has typically been sacrificed to meet budget performance conditionalities, as evidenced by reductions in existing programmes or delays in implementing or expanding new social protection initiatives (United Nations, 2004c).

Even in some developed countries, social protection coverage is far from universal and benefits are generally inadequate. Furthermore, the trend in a number of high-income countries is towards the effective reduction of welfare and other income-support benefits. Other measures are being implemented to privatize certain social insurance schemes such as pensions and medical plans. These reform efforts are spurred, at least in part, by growing cost pressures arising in connection with population ageing, changing family structures, increasingly expensive medical care and persistent unemployment. However, the drive to make social security systems more efficient by adopting a market-oriented approach and by expanding the role of the private sector in pension and health-care provision has undermined social solidarity. Of particular concern are the increased inequalities generated by gender discrimination in private systems owing to the lack of solidarity and inter-gender transfers to correct for imbalances in pension contribution levels (Mesa-Lago, 2004). Overall, the effects of these reform measures on people and the economy are mixed but tend to be more heavily concentrated on the negative side, effectively reinforcing the notion that the State continues to play a crucial role in social protection.

Patterns of intervention

Different approaches have been tried in efforts to reach beneficiary groups more efficiently, with the choice often coming down to a universal versus a more targeted approach. Universalism involves guaranteeing all members of society certain fundamental protections and benefits that are necessary for full participation in society. Universalism is closely linked to the principle of solidarity, and individuals are expected to share in the financing of services according to their economic capacity, mainly through taxation. Serious obstacles to the universal application of social benefits have included the shortage of resources, the lack of agreement on priorities and problems of implementation. Targeting involves funnelling protections and benefits to selected groups of individuals based on real or perceived need or as a means of gaining political patronage. Given the scarcity of public resources, particularly in developing countries and during periods of economic adjustment and times of crisis, targeting is often viewed as the better option, as it is more cost-effective and increases the likelihood that social services will reach those who need them most, with minimal slippage to the non-needy. An example of a targeted programme is one in which income transfers are conditional upon children remaining in school and receiving essential health-care services; such an initiative is intended to improve lifelong income-earning capacity and can be an important part of a more equitable welfare state (World Bank, 2004b).

Many countries have experimented with other patterns of intervention aside from targeting, including expanding the role of the private sector in the delivery of social services. The shift in focus from public to private institutions has occurred as a result of the confluence of several factors, including pressure to liberalize the economy, the relative scarcity of public resources and the low quality of public service provision. In many countries public social services have been privatized or outsourced to private contractors. In other countries, the provision of education, health care and other services has remained in the public domain, but user fees have been introduced. The transfer of responsibility from the public to the private sector has also been observed in social protection, often under privatization schemes, in which case social assistance generally declines and public health programmes are scaled back, resulting in a weakening of the social protection system.

Different combinations of public and private participation have been developed to facilitate the provision of a wide range of social services and benefits. With a school voucher system, for example, public funding is used to provide private education to children from poor families (United Nations Development Programme, 2003). When private participation is a component of social service provision and the goal is to attain universality and to provide benefits for disadvantaged groups, it is essential to ensure that exclusion does not occur. Experience has shown that if public-private participation is not properly designed and monitored, access can be seriously limited, and some people may be excluded. A stronger regulatory framework is therefore needed to guarantee access to social services, with legal mechanisms for preventing or halting practices that exclude or discriminate against certain groups. Even under the best of circumstances, private sector participation in the administration and delivery of social services and benefits systems cannot replace the public provision of these services.

Notwithstanding efforts to engage the private sector, the State and the public sector continue to bear primary responsibility for the provision of most

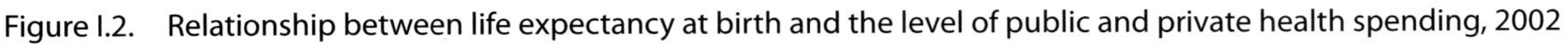

Figure I.2. Relationship between life expectancy at birth and the level of public and private health spending, 2002

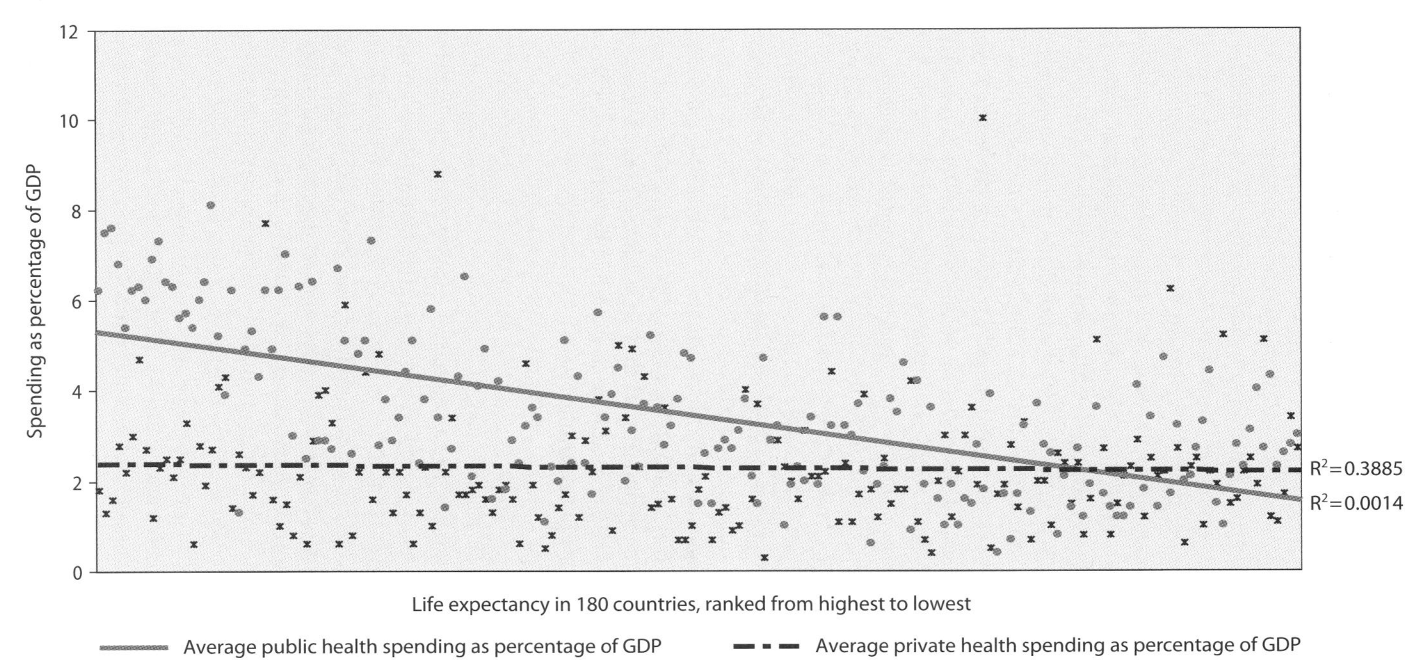

Source: United Nations Development Programme, *Human Development Report 2004* (http://hdr.undp.org/statistics/data; accessed 23 May 2005)

social services, and for ensuring that these services are made available to all, especially the poorest segments of the population. The efficacy of the public system is clearly illustrated in the strong relationship between public sector health spending and life expectancy, as depicted in figure I.2. Those countries that have had the greatest success in increasing life expectancy (notably Australia, Canada, Iceland, Japan, Spain and Sweden) have maintained high rates of public health spending, equivalent to between 5 and 8 percent of gross domestic product (GDP), while private sector health spending has been much lower. The relationship between life expectancy and private spending on health is weak in all countries, with the exception of a few outliers (Cambodia, Lebanon and the United States of America), where private sector health spending as a percentage of GDP is particularly high. In contrast, the relationship between public health spending and life expectancy is strong, with differences in the levels of public sector spending on health accounting for close to 40 per cent of the variation in life expectancy by country. This evidence should be given careful consideration, especially in an era in which developing country Governments are under substantial pressure to reduce public sector spending for social services in favour of private spending.

A proper balance between public and private sector involvement in the delivery of social services should be sought to ensure that the principles of universality, solidarity and social inclusion are preserved. In order to promote greater equality, the public management of services should be characterized by high levels of efficiency and transparency. Non-governmental organizations (NGOs) often play an important role in facilitating the achievement of these and other relevant standards, as they help fill the gaps in the provision of public services and also constitute a strong force in promoting community concerns, especially for poor people.

Conclusion

The key to reducing poverty in a sustainable manner, particularly with an eye to promoting social justice, is to focus on building a fairer and more equitable society. Economic growth alone is not a panacea, as the level of inequality can be a determining factor in the impact growth has on poverty reduction. Overcoming inequalities requires an investment in people, with priority given to enhancing educational attainment, skill development, health care and overall well-being, and to expanding and improving opportunities for quality employment. Equal attention must be given to the socio-political dimensions of poverty, and a serious commitment is needed to ensure that discrimination is eliminated and its consequences are addressed, that the equal protection of human rights is guaranteed, and that a better balance is achieved in the distribution of political power and the level of representation among all stakeholders. Accordingly, people need to be empowered to voice their concerns and participate more actively in decision-making processes.

The role of the State in reducing inequality remains critical, notwithstanding reform efforts aimed at turning over responsibility for social programmes to the private sector. Ensuring equal access for all to public services—particularly education and health care, which are aimed at expanding opportunities and capabilities—is fundamental to reducing the intergenerational transmission of poverty and inequality. Thus, the principles of universality, solidarity and social inclusion should continue to guide the delivery of social services.

The World Summit for Social Development established a common foundation for social policy reform processes that has guided efforts to address the inequality trends that deepened with the implementation of the structural adjustment programmes in the 1980s and 1990s. The Copenhagen Declaration emphasizes the need to attain universal and equitable access to education and primary health care. While focusing on these important factors and principles in redressing inequality, it is essential not to lose sight of the general values governing equality of access, the importance of culture and tolerance, the people-centred approach to development, and the full development of human resources.

The principles of equality should be at the centre of social and economic policy-making to ensure that economic growth is conducive to social development, stability, fair competition and ethical conduct (United Nations, 1995, chap. I, para. 12b). In view of the prevailing world social situation, characterized as it is by rampant inequality, it is essential that policy makers heed the challenges posed by the inequality predicament. As the present analysis indicates thus far, and as the ensuing chapters make abundantly clear, doing otherwise would be highly counterproductive.

Notes

1 See the annex containing the 10 commitments of the World Summit for Social Development.

Chapter II
A spotlight on inequality: the informal economy

An examination of the informal economy, contrasted with the formal economy, highlights the importance of focusing on inequality in the pursuit of more equitable and just social development. Those who are part of the formal economy generally fall among the "haves" in society, as they are more likely to earn decent wages, receive job-related benefits, have secure employment contracts and be covered by relevant laws and regulations. In contrast, those in the informal economy are typically among the "have nots"; they are often excluded from various legal protections and are prevented from accessing basic benefits or enjoying the fundamental rights afforded those in the formal economy. Given that most poor people work informally, the presence, and indeed the recent expansion, of the informal economy in many countries has major implications for reducing poverty and inequality.

Being in the formal economy implies both rights (protections) and responsibilities, whereas in the informal economy there is little of either, and the resulting imbalance contributes to inequality. On the side of rights and protections, those in the informal economy are generally not covered by national labour laws, including safety and health regulations, and are not eligible for social security benefits, pensions or other forms of social protection. In addition, informal workers and employers are usually deprived of the right to organize and bargain collectively.

On the side of responsibilities, workers and employers in the informal economy generally do not pay income or payroll taxes on earnings, or costs such as licence fees, since their activities are unregulated and undocumented. With the tax burden thus unevenly distributed, another form of inequality is perpetuated. Workers and employers in the formal economy are left to shoulder the lion's share of the tax bill, while those in the informal economy are largely exempt from this responsibility. Those in the informal economy who are capable of paying, but do not do so, enjoy a competitive advantage over those in the formal economy. These uncollected tax revenues are likely to translate into a lower quality and quantity of public services for the poor and vulnerable in society, further perpetuating the cycle of inequality.

An objective comparison of the formal and informal economies reveals myriad inequalities, ranging from wage, benefit and gender disparities to sizeable imbalances in the tax burden. These glaring differentials aside, greater focus on the informal economy is warranted simply because it accounts for a significant share, and in some settings even a majority, of total economic activity in a number of developing countries. Arguably, if adequate attention is not given to the informal economy, little can be done to remedy the conditions created by inequality and injustice throughout the world.

A brief overview of the informal economy

A precise definition of the term "informal economy" is elusive, though there have been numerous attempts over the years to arrive at a working definition. Without a common definition, however, it is important to bear in mind that measurements will vary according to the way the term is defined. Essentially, the informal economy can be described in terms of those who work in it (employment status), or in terms of the activities that take place in it (type of economic activity).[1]

Different measurements result from assessments based on these two different approaches. The size of the informal economy is measured in terms of employment; using the broader approach to identify the types of economic activity, it is measured as a share of GDP. Both methods of assessment indicate that the informal economy has increased rapidly in recent decades in both developing and industrialized countries, and that it contributes significantly to the overall economy in most countries. Table II.1 highlights the rapid expansion of the informal economy in selected countries. Because the data are based on national definitions, they are comparable only within individual countries over time.

Informal employment accounts for between one half and three quarters of non-agricultural employment in the majority of developing countries. The share of informal workers in the non-agricultural labour force ranges from 48 per cent in North Africa and 51 per cent in Latin America and the Caribbean to 65 per cent in Asia and 78 per cent in sub-Saharan Africa[2] (International Labour Organization, 2002b).

Sectors other than agriculture tend to be the primary employers of informal workers, in part owing to migration from rural to urban areas, which produces a large pool of workers lacking the skills necessary for employment in the formal economy. Those with limited skills are the most vulnerable in the informal economy as they are more likely to work under inhumane conditions and accept low wages. Although a large proportion of those working in the informal economy are fully employed, it is a source of work for many in the labour force who are underemployed in the formal economy or have been unable to secure and retain jobs there. Though the formal and informal economies may overlap in some areas, deep divisions remain, further segmenting society, increasing social tensions and deterring the poor from participating in the development process (Economic Commission for Latin America and the Caribbean, 2005b). Informal trade, mainly street trade, comprises 30 to 50 per cent of urban informal employment (Charmes, 1998).

Workers in the informal economy constitute an eclectic group that includes street vendors, rickshaw pullers, home-based garment workers and casual day labourers. Employment status varies; in the informal economy there are non-wage workers (independent workers), including employers who are owners of informal enterprises and self-employed workers, as well as wage workers (dependent workers), including domestic workers, homeworkers and

Table II.1. Size and growth of the informal economy[a] in selected countries, by sex

Country	Year	Number (thousands)			Women per 100 men	Informal employment as percentage of employment		
		Total	Men	Women		Total	Men	Women
Kyrgyzstan	1994	140.0	..	..	..	8.2	..	..
	1999	194.1	118.8	75.3	63	24.9	28.5	20.8
Lithuania	1998	154.2	86.1	68.1	79	48.5	46.9	50.7
	2000	201.6	116.6	85.0	73	72.0	71.9	72.2
Mali	1989	383.0	176.8	206.1	117	78.6	67.6	91.5
	1996	1 176.1	485.6	690.2	142	94.1	91.0	96.4
Mexico	1991	6 328.4	3 750.0	2 578.4	69	30.9	29.5	33.1
	1999	9 141.6	5 693.8	3 447.7	61	31.9	32.7	30.7
Slovakia	1994	362.0	276.3	85.7	31	17.6	23.2	9.9
	1999	450.0	343.5	106.5	31	23.0	30.5	12.9
	1998	1 431.0	1 001.0	430.0	43	9.2	11.6	6.2
South Africa	1999	2 705.0	1 162.0	1 544.0	133	26.1	19.3	35.5
	2001	3 319.0	1 572.0	1 746.0	111	31.0	25.7	38.2

Source: International Labour Organization, Bureau of Statistics, based on published national data.
[a] National definition.

employees of informal enterprises. Outside of agriculture, self-employment accounts for 60 to 70 per cent of informal work in developing countries, while wage-based employment accounts for only 30 to 40 per cent (International Labour Organization, 2002b). What binds the members of this heterogeneous group of workers together is the lack of secure employment contracts, work-related benefits, social protection and a "voice" (representation).

According to estimates based on data from the International Labour Organization (ILO), in 2003 a total of 1.39 billion people, or 49.7 per cent of the world's workers, were unable to lift themselves and their families above the poverty threshold of US$ 2 per day. Even more striking, nearly one in four workers in the developing world (23.3 per cent) were living on less than US$ 1 per day (International Labour Organization, 2005c). The majority of workers with very low incomes are likely to be found in the informal economy, where average wages are lower. Not all workers in the informal economy are among the working poor; nonetheless, an estimate of the working poor can be viewed as an approximation of those working in the informal economy whose earnings are very low (International Labour Organization, 2005c). It also stands to reason that because workers in the informal economy lack rights, protections and representation, they are more likely to remain trapped in poverty.

In addition to earning lower average wages, informal workers are seldom provided with social security coverage or other forms of social protection by either their employers or the Government. The lack of social protection—encompassing opportunities, resources and services such as health care, pensions, education, skill development, training and childcare—contributes further to the social exclusion of these workers. Part of the difficulty in extending social security coverage to informal workers stems from the limitations inherent in raising revenues and collecting contributions from workers with minimal earnings; the general absence of a direct employer-employee relationship is another factor. Efforts to extend social security protection to informal workers are growing, however; in India, for example, there is an initiative to tax the aggregate output of designated industries in order to finance benefits for all workers in those industries (Chen, Jhabvala and Lund, 2002).

It is important to note that although wages and benefits are generally lower in the informal economy than in the formal economy, significant variations exist even within the informal economy. Wages tend to decline in the informal economy across the spectrum of employment activity; employers earn the most, with remuneration gradually falling for self-employed and casual wage workers and continuing to decline for subcontract workers. Women tend to fall into the last three categories, and are over-represented among subcontract workers and under-represented among employers (Women in Informal Employment: Globalizing and Organizing, 2004c). Add to that the fact that more women than men tend to work informally, and the level of economic inequality between men and women becomes even more apparent.

Overall, about 60 per cent of women working outside of agriculture in developing countries are informally employed (International Labour Organization, 2002b). Home-based work and street vending are common among women in informal employment. Myriad problems confront homeworkers, among them long hours with low pay and poor working conditions; exclusion from national labour laws; work instability; the lack of the right to organize and bargain collectively; and the absence of work-related benefits such as pensions, insurance, safety and health protection, and paid leave. An outgrowth of these conditions is that children are often required to work to supplement the family's income (Women in Informal Employment: Globalizing and Organizing, 2004b).

Few women employ others, and few men are industrial outworkers or homeworkers. Differences are also pronounced within the same industry. For example, men traders generally have larger operations and deal in non-perishable goods, whereas women traders usually have smaller operations and deal in food items (Chen, Jhabvala and Lund, 2002). As this suggests, the link between working in the informal economy and being poor is stronger for women than for men, which can be associated with the growing trend towards the "feminization of poverty". Exacerbating the situation is the fact that women are frequently not given the legal right to own or hold land, and even where this right is recognized, there is a sizeable gap between legal recognition and their effective access to land (United Nations Research Institute for Social Development, 2005). All of these factors contribute to the higher rates of unemployment, underemployment and low-wage informal employment among women.

Informal economic activities exist along a continuum, ranging from survival-driven work to stable, resilient enterprises, to dynamic, efficient and growing businesses. The informal economy accounts for a significant share of GDP and gross national income (GNI) in almost all countries, particularly those in the developing world. According to a study of the informal economy in 110 countries, its average size as a share of official GNI in 2000 ranged from 18 per cent in OECD countries to 38 per cent in transition countries and 41 per cent in developing countries. Among specific regions, the informal economy accounted for an average of 42 per cent of GNP in Africa, 26 per cent in Asia and 41 per cent in Latin America in 1999/2000 (Schneider, 2002).

The same study indicates that the informal economy has been growing in those OECD countries included in the analysis; their collective share increased from 13 to 17 per cent of GDP between 1989/90 and 1999/2000 (using unweighted averages), with signs of a slowdown in growth during the second half of this period. In developed market economies, informal employment is characterized as non-standard work, and includes part-time and temporary work, self-employment and various forms of casual day labour or contract work, all of which typically offer limited work-related benefits and social protection.

A subsequent study released in 2002 estimated the contribution of informal enterprises to GDP in 26 developing countries. The preliminary results of the study showed a fairly wide range at the regional level, with averages of 27 per cent for North Africa, 29 per cent for Latin America, 31 per cent for Asia and 41 per cent for sub-Saharan Africa. Among the countries represented in the study, Mexico reported the lowest relative share (13 per cent) and Ghana the highest (58 per cent). The disparities are at least partially attributable to the differences in methods used by countries in preparing estimates on the informal economy (International Labour Organization, 2002b).

The attraction of the informal economy

With all of its disadvantages, why does the informal economy comprise such a significant and growing portion of the total economy, particularly in developing countries? One essential reason is the lack of other options. As the economically active population increases, the formal economy is unable to absorb all those seeking work, especially in the developing world. Many turn to the informal economy because they cannot find jobs or are unable to start businesses in the formal economy. For a large proportion of the working-age population, particularly in developing countries, participation in the informal economy is not a choice but a means of survival. For those compelled to engage in survival activities, the informal economy offers ease of entry. Participants can avail themselves of local resources, operations are usually run on a small scale and are therefore more manageable, and minimal capital investment is required. Moreover, education, skill and technology requirements are generally nominal, enabling poorly educated and untrained workers to gain a foothold in the workforce.

It is important to recognize that not all individuals involved in the informal economy are there because they have no other choice. For those who have built their own businesses, the informal economy is attractive because it offers the possibility of wealth accumulation without taxation and regulation. For others, the informal economy is appealing because it offers considerable flexibility, including part-time and temporary opportunities (Chen, Jhabvala and Lund, 2002). Furthermore, the informal economy helps many people cultivate their entrepreneurial spirit and acts as a breeding ground for developing business acumen, innovation and important job-related skills.

In developed countries in particular, an attraction of the informal economy is that it enables enterprises to avoid paying income taxes, social security taxes and other wage-related taxes. Employers also save money by circumventing health, safety and environmental regulations and by disregarding intellectual property rights. A cross-country comparison among OECD countries showed that the more expensive and more complicated the taxes and regulations of a country were, the larger the informal economy was as a share of GDP (The Economist, 2004).

Overall, these findings lead to the following conclusions: (a) the informal economy tends to be larger in areas in which the burdens of tax and social security contributions are comparatively heavy; the same is true in settings with relatively high levels of State regulatory activity; and (b) as the difference between the total cost of labour and after-tax wages increases, so does the incentive to work in the informal economy (Schneider, 2002).

In some cases, however, informal entrepreneurs are required to pay taxes, and even find themselves at a competitive disadvantage with larger, formal operators. For example, when corporate taxes are lowered to assist businesses, larger corporations in the formal economy are able to benefit from the tax cuts, whereas informal entrepreneurs are not. In some areas, city councils send out tax collectors to ensure that daily market fees are paid by street vendors, whether or not they are registered with the local authority. Indirect taxes from city councils can also come in the form of fines and bribes, so it can be in the interest of the city government to keep informal enterprises informal (Chen, Jhabvala and Lund, 2002).

Aside from the competitive advantages and disadvantages associated with tax collection in the informal economy, there is the impact on State revenues to consider. As the share of the informal economy in the total economy increases, State tax revenues inevitably decline, leading to a deterioration in the quantity and quality of public goods and services. To compensate for the slump in tax receipts, Governments can either raise tax rates in the formal economy, running the risk of encouraging more enterprises to move into the informal economy, or scale back public services. Under either scenario, imbalances are created and the level of inequality increases, affecting the vulnerable and disadvantaged most severely in the long run.

In a kind of ironic twist, labour law has also played a key role in increasing the attraction of the informal economy for many. The essential logic or purpose behind labour law is to moderate the inherent disequilibrium between labour and capital, balancing interests in such a way as to provide security for working families while at the same time not stifling entrepreneurial dynamism (Trebilcock, 2004). The trouble is that labour law has not kept pace with changes in the labour market or responded effectively to globalization, and legal and administrative requirements have raised the threshold of entry into the formal economy, placing it beyond the reach of many people (International Labour Organization, 2003). Employers or entrepreneurs who face too many legal obstacles to hiring or starting a business in the formal economy turn instead to the informal economy. Reforming labour laws to make them more responsive to changing conditions can help slow the rising trend towards informal employment, and in so doing re-establish greater equilibrium between labour and capital.

Reasons for the growth of the informal economy

For many years, development experts held the belief that an emphasis on economic growth would promote overall development, including a natural decline in the informal economy, and ultimately lead to a reduction in poverty. Over the past several decades, however, developing countries have witnessed the rapid expansion of the informal economy, rather than the synchronous decline that had been expected to accompany economic growth and industrial development. Exploring the reasons for this increase provides insight into the impact that economic growth, competitiveness and liberalization policies can have on inequality.

As touched upon previously, the informal economy has a strong and growing appeal despite its inherent disadvantages. While the reasons for its expansion in recent years are manifold, the three principal factors explaining the increase in most countries are patterns of economic growth, economic restructuring and economic crisis, and the restructuring of production chains in response to global competition (Carr and Chen, 2002).

Patterns of economic growth. Some countries have registered little or no economic growth, while others have experienced "jobless growth", or capital-intensive growth. When not enough jobs are being generated for all those seeking work in the formal economy, some will be compelled to secure employment in the informal economy. Often the labour market is affected by changes in skill requirements. With the relatively rapid growth in the high-technology sector, for example, more high-skilled than low-skilled jobs have been created in many economies, and those who have not acquired the skills needed to compete in the evolving labour market may find that their only option is the informal economy.

A more positive aspect of the growth patterns contributing to the expansion of the informal economy has been the proliferation of small and micro businesses. These enterprises, which frequently operate in the informal economy, are in many cases more dynamic than their larger, formal counterparts, making them the engines of growth and job creation in some industries, regions and countries.

Economic restructuring and economic crisis. Evidence indicates that the informal economy expands during periods of economic adjustment or transition, as experienced by the countries of the former Union of Soviet Socialist Republics; and during economic crises, as experienced in Latin America and South-East Asia in the 1990s. During periods of economic adjustment, retrenched workers move into the informal economy in order to survive. With the downsizing of the public sector and the closure of public enterprises, particularly in connection with structural adjustment programmes, laid-off workers have few alternatives available. As social protection programmes such as unemployment insurance and pensions are inadequate or even non-existent in many countries, workers cannot afford to remain openly unemployed. Many turn to the informal economy as a way to support themselves and their families; in effect, it becomes a kind of safety net. People also gravitate to the informal economy when they need to supplement the family income in response to inflation or cutbacks in public services (International Labour Organization, 2002b). Even with the onset of macroeconomic stabilization and economic growth following the period of economic adjustment, the informal economy tends to remain, or even continues to grow, especially if there are no appropriate institutions or policies in place to counter its expansion (Johnson, Kaufmann and Schleifler, 1997).

The restructuring of production chains in response to global competition. The fundamental changes made to enhance global competitiveness have also played a major role in the expansion of the informal economy. Global trade and investment patterns tend to favour capital, especially large transnational corporations that can readily move capital and goods across borders, and to constitute a disadvantage for labour, especially low-skilled workers who may find it difficult or impossible to migrate. While the liberalization of trade and capital has been encouraged, little has been done to facilitate the free flow of labour across national boundaries. In fact, many countries are trying to tighten their borders and limit the influx of migrant workers. As a result of these developments, the widening of skill-based income differentials has become a worldwide phenomenon (Ocampo, 2002b).

In an effort to increase their global competitiveness, investors are shifting production to countries with lower labour costs and increasing their reliance on more informal employment arrangements, including "flexible specialization". Flexible arrangements usually involve an erosion of employment standards, as workers are neither afforded minimum wage rates nor given assurances of continued work, and rarely receive benefits. In many cases, such arrangements amount to no more than piece-rate or casual work. The drive to cut costs has led to the radical restructuring of production and distribution in many key industries in favour of outsourcing or subcontracting through global commodity chains. These chains begin with large companies, which in some cases focus only on the design and marketing of their products and subcontract all manufacturing and production responsibilities to suppliers in low-wage countries. In turn, these suppliers contract with small, informal production units, which further contract out work orders to isolated, informal workers. These workers at the end of the chain are typically paid very low wages, and many, such as industrial homeworkers, have to absorb the non-wage costs of production. The employment situation is so precarious in many areas that large number of informal workers, particularly the poor and vulnerable, are compelled to accept any terms offered. In segments of the garment industry, for example, companies will not provide workers with secure employment contracts, giving them only the option of working as home-based subcontractors (Chen, Jhabvala and Lund, 2002). Under these circumstances, it is not only that firms in the formal economy are *unable* to absorb labour; they are also *unwilling* to do so.

Globalization also favours large companies that can capture new markets quickly and easily over small and micro enterprises that have difficulty gaining an understanding of and access to emerging markets. Self-employment also becomes more precarious because individual producers and traders are apt to lose their market niche. With globalization, low-skill workers and petty producers lose much of their bargaining power and face increased competition, putting them at a further disadvantage.

Globalization does present opportunities as well as threats; however, many in the informal economy find it difficult to avail themselves of the opportunities because they are cut off from the benefits typically enjoyed by participants in the mainstream formal economy, including access to loans and information about prices, the quality and sources of goods, and potential markets and customers (Chen, Jhabvala and Lund, 2002). The self-employed (and women in general) often lack access to credit, training, technologies and market information. These individuals also face competition from those dealing with imported products in the domestic market or from larger formal units (in export markets), and sometimes have to move into other, less profitable areas of the informal economy, perhaps engaging in petty trading or piecework either at home or in a factory with low wages and under poor working conditions (Carr and Chen, 2002).

Further compounding the difficulties, the sustained expansion of the informal economy eventually results in overcrowding, generating greater internal competition. Added competition exerts downward pressure on earnings within this segment of the economy, making it even more difficult for people to earn a living, regardless of how much they work or how many family members are brought in to help out.

Linkages between the formal and informal economies

Though the formal and informal economies move along separate tracks, they are nonetheless interrelated and characterized by numerous intricate linkages. What has gradually emerged is a continuum of production and employment relations, with the formal and informal economies becoming more interdependent than distinct. The question is whether the linkages are benign, exploitative or mutually advantageous (Carr and Chen, 2002). Once this relationship is better defined, the challenge turns to enhancing the positive linkages in order to ensure the promotion of decent work in both economies.

The experience of a number of key export industries (producers of garments, leather goods, textiles, sports shoes, carpets and electronics) can be used to illustrate the linkages between the formal and informal economies. A high percentage of the labour force in these industries are employed under informal arrangements, with many working in export processing zones, in sweatshops or out of their homes. What links them to the formal economy is a global commodity chain, a network that connects the various labour, production and distribution processes contributing to the manufacture and placement of a single commodity or product. There are two main types of global value chains that represent the full range of activities required to take a product from conception to end-use and beyond. With buyer-driven chains, such as those found in the footwear and garment sectors, retailers govern production. With producer-driven chains, which characterize the automobile and electronics sectors, large manufacturers govern the process. Every link in the chain, from the production of inputs to the sale of final products, is controlled by powerful buyers or producers. Those at the bottom of the chain, namely home-based workers in the informal economy, typically benefit least from these arrangements (Women in Informal Employment: Globalizing and Organizing, 2004a).

A shift has occurred in global production and distribution with the more widespread adoption of the just-in-time inventory management and control system, or "lean retailing", which is characterized by the absence of a large amount of stock on hand or on order. In the garment industry, for example, the supply turnaround time is short, and a competitive order-to-delivery lead time can only be maintained if the subcontractors furnishing the goods are located relatively close to the main markets in Europe and North America. In response to such market demands, there has been an increase in home-based work in countries in close proximity to these markets, precipitating a decline in the large-scale garment industry in Asia. As the industry becomes more dispersed and volatile, homeworkers are less likely to receive the pay due them or to be notified when their contracts end, deepening their experience of economic inequality. The cumulative result of these trends is that the informal economy, despite being considered incompatible with economic growth and industrialization, has expanded considerably in both developed and developing countries (Carr and Chen, 2002).

As mentioned previously, the rising competitive pressures accompanying globalization have compelled companies and employers to seek more flexible work arrangements in order to cut costs. Consequently, reliance on subcontracting has increased, with home-based work constituting an especially attractive option. The proliferation of information technology, including the Internet, has also facilitated the movement towards home-based work, as larger numbers of clerical, technical and professional workers are able to work at home rather than at a job site. This shift allows employers to save on rent, utilities and other costs associated with maintaining a workplace.

Home-based self-employment has also grown, largely in response to the contraction of the formal economy, as many people have had no choice but to explore informal work options on their own. While some may find it advantageous to work at home, there are some notable disadvantages for the home-based self-employed; in particular, these individuals often remain outside the information loop and lack access to financial markets and the capacity to compete in product markets.

Some of the more common home-based work activities include rolling cigarettes; stitching garments; providing laundry or childcare services; assembling electrical plugs or electronic components; entering, processing or analysing data; and providing professional or technical services to individuals or businesses (International Labour Organization, 2002b). Not included in this category are those engaged in unpaid housework or paid domestic work. Wages and working conditions can vary dramatically among home-based workers, depending on the type of activity performed and the characteristics of the informal economy in a particular country.

Generally, the lowest-paid and most economically disadvantaged home-based workers are industrial homeworkers, who engage in activities such as garment production for businesses, typically on a piece-rate basis. Their numbers are significant and growing; industrial homeworkers currently comprise 30 to 60 per cent of the workforce in the garment, textile and footwear industries (Chen, Sebstad and O'Connell, 1999). A stumbling block to improving the wages and working conditions of industrial homeworkers is the difficulty in determining whether the employer is the intermediary that directly places the work order, the supplier that contracts with the intermediary, the manufacturer that obtains goods from the supplier or the retailer that sells the finished product. Without a clear indication of who the employer is, it is also unclear who should be responsible for protecting the rights and benefits of these workers.

Linkages between the formal and informal economies can also affect productivity growth. As competitive pressures in the formal economy intensify, more firms have an incentive to move into the informal or "grey" economy. "Grey" firms tend to be small, which helps them stay under the radar of tax authorities, and they prefer to stay that way to continue avoiding taxation. Remaining in the informal economy comes at a price, however, as these intentionally small enterprises tend to be less efficient, which serves to undermine productivity growth and ultimately the overall economic growth of the country. Nevertheless, labour-intensive industries such as retailing are inclined to stay fragmented and inefficient because the informal operators perceive that any productivity benefits deriving from an increase in scale would be offset by the increased tax obligations in the formal economy. A recent study suggests that broadening the tax base, cutting tax rates and improving enforcement might bring more businesses into the formal economy, indirectly raising productivity rates (Farrell, 2004).

It has been argued that employment creation can actually hinder productivity growth. If the jobs created are not decent and productive and do not provide a sufficient income, they will not have a favourable impact on the demand side of the economy (International Labour Organization, 2005c). In order for economic growth to be sustainable in a country, there has to be a domestic market for the goods and services produced. If not enough people in the country have sufficient earnings to buy the domestically produced goods and services, economic growth is bound to stagnate. This supports the argument that decent work and productivity growth have to accompany GDP growth; under these conditions, economic growth can lead to poverty reduction.

Conclusion

For most workers and many employers in the informal economy, the negative aspects of participation—not being recognized, registered, regulated or protected under labour laws or covered under social protection schemes—far outweigh any perceived advantages. What the ILO refers to as "decent work deficits" are more pronounced in the informal economy than elsewhere. Working in the informal economy often implies unsafe and unhealthy working conditions, long working hours with insufficient and unsteady compensation, low skill and productivity levels, and a general lack of access to information, markets, finance, training and technology (International Labour Organization, 2002a).

Another important factor perpetuating inequality is that those in the informal economy often do not have secure property rights, which restricts or blocks their access to capital and credit, thereby limiting their ability to expand and grow their businesses. Informal workers and employers also tend to have difficulty gaining access to the judicial system to enforce contracts, leaving them without any means of seeking redress and thus more vulnerable to harassment, exploitation, abuse, corruption and bribery. A coherent legal and judicial framework is needed to ensure that property rights are secured and respected so that assets can be turned into productive capital.

While efforts should be made to address the negative aspects of informal work, or to reduce the decent work deficits, it is important not to destroy the capacity of the informal economy to provide a livelihood or to develop entrepreneurial potential. Rather than regarding all informal work as negative, it is useful to view it as existing somewhere along the "continuum of decent work". At one end of the continuum are unprotected, unregulated survivalist jobs, and at the other end are decent, protected and regulated jobs. The goal, ultimately, is to enhance the linkages between the informal and the formal economies, and to ensure that there is decent work all along the continuum—where workers have rights, protection and a voice—and not necessarily focus on "formalizing the informal". Ideally, there should be movement upward along the continuum so that there is not only job growth but improvements in the quality of jobs as well (Trebilcock, 2004). Efforts to reduce the decent work deficits in the informal economy and ensure that people are both empowered and protected will simultaneously contribute to poverty reduction.

Traditionally, it has been difficult for workers and employers in the informal economy to secure membership in, and therefore enjoy the services of, larger employer and worker organizations, leaving them with little hope that their rights at work will be acknowledged or respected. Women and youth, who make up the majority of workers in the informal economy, are particularly vulnerable, as they tend to have no voice or representation; the same is true for home-based workers, whose isolation from other workers means that they typically have little bargaining power relative to their employers or other workers. There are signs of progress, however. Some important players in an expanding international movement to support those working in the informal economy include the following: Women in Informal Employment: Globalizing and Organizing (Women in Informal Employment: Globalizing and Organizing, 2004c), a global research and policy analysis network of women in the informal economy; StreetNet, an international alliance of street vendors; and HomeNet, a worldwide alliance of home-based workers. The emergence of these and similar groups is a positive step towards providing excluded and often exploited workers with representation and a voice.

The report of the World Commission on the Social Dimension of Globalization stresses the importance of advancing the huge informal economy along the decent work continuum, emphasizing that this is an essential part of the overriding effort to achieve a more inclusive globalization. It is suggested that this might be accomplished by ensuring that workers' rights, including property rights, are clearly established and consistently respected, and by increasing productivity and access to markets for informal producers (International Labour Organization, 2004). Enormous strides can be made in resolving the inequality predicament if steps are taken to ensure that the informal economy becomes an integral part of an expanding, dynamic economy that provides decent jobs, incomes and protection, as well as fair and competitive trade opportunities within the international system.

Notes

1 For various definitions of the informal economy, see the following: International Labour Organization (ILO), "Report of the International Conference of Labour Statisticians" (Geneva, 1993); ILO, "Conclusions concerning decent work and the informal economy", adopted by the International Labour Conference at its ninetieth session, Geneva, 3-20 June 2002 (see the ILC Provisional Record, No. 25, para. 3); and Friedrich Schneider, "Size and measurement of the informal economy in 110 countries around the world", World Bank Working Paper (Washington, D.C., July 2002), p. 3, referring to definitions used by Feige (1989, 1994), Schneider (1994), and Frey and Pommerehne (1984).

2 Excluding South Africa.

Chapter III
Trends and patterns of inequality

The issue of global economic inequality and the underlying economic forces contributing to its evolution constitute one of the most controversial aspects of economic discourse in recent years. Until recently, economic indicators dominated much of the discussion about global inequality, reflecting the priority given to policies promoting economic growth as a panacea for development ills. Now, however, greater attention is being paid to the non-economic indicators of inequality. Similar to the shift that has taken place in the debate on poverty, the debate on inequality has come to reflect a broader conceptualization of the subject in which the focus is not exclusively on measurable economic indicators.

As non-economic aspects of inequality become more widely recognized, the distinctions that will inevitably be drawn between economic and non-economic inequality may create a false dichotomy between phenomena that are intricately related. Inequality is complex and multidimensional and is manifested in various forms at the community, national and global levels. Individuals, groups and countries that lack opportunities at one level generally lack opportunities at other levels as well. For example, in societies with high levels of income inequality, those who control the resources also tend to control the political system, and those without access to either are neglected. Likewise, the global marketplace operates to the advantage of richer countries; poor countries are less likely to benefit from globalization and are more vulnerable to its risks and failures (Birdsall, 2002).

This interdependence is one aspect of a complex structural relationship between economic and non-economic inequalities both within and between countries; the many, varied linkages are impossible to isolate, complicating efforts to develop solutions. A key feature of the structural relationship between economic and non-economic inequality is that both are often characterized by inequality under the law and inequality of opportunities and conditions—issues highlighted at the World Summit for Social Development.

The present chapter describes the magnitude and summarizes the trends and patterns of selected aspects of economic and non-economic inequality at the national and global levels. It begins with a review of trends in economic inequality, measured in terms of income distribution, monetary poverty, and employment. The chapter then summarizes the various trends associated with selected non-economic aspects of inequality, including health, mortality, malnutrition and education.

It is important to note at the outset that while considerable evidence exists with regard to trends in inequality at both the national and international levels, data remain incomplete. This is particularly true for developing countries and applies to both economic and non-economic indicators of inequality. Any interpretation of the levels and trends presented in the sections below (especially short-term trends) should take these data limitations into account.

Economic aspects of inequality

Income inequality between countries

Recent analyses of global inequality patterns suggest that income and consumption inequality between countries has been relatively stable during the past 50 years (Berry and Serieux, 2002). However, in general terms, measurements of economic growth indicate that there has been an expansion in world income since the 1980s. This overall trend has primarily been driven by the sustained and rapid growth of the economy in China and the continuous, though more moderate, economic growth in India; both countries have played a crucial role in the expansion of the world economy in the past two decades. While these and some of the other economies in Asia have grown fairly rapidly, North America and Western Europe have registered only moderate levels of economic growth. Following a slowdown in the 1980s and a recession in the early 1990s, the economy in Eastern Europe resumed growth during the mid-1990s. Most countries in Central and South America and the Middle East experienced negative economic growth during the 1980s, and growth rates in sub-Saharan Africa remained negative during most of the 1980s and 1990s (Berry and Serieux, 2002).

Although the issue remains subject to considerable debate, there has probably been a moderate improvement in the overall world distribution of income during the past two decades (Berry and Serieux, 2004; Sala-i-Martin, 2002). Upon further analysis, however, the picture that emerges is not quite so positive. First, most of the improvement in the distribution of world income can be explained by the rapid economic growth in China and, to a lesser extent, India (see figure III.1), with a good part of the shift reflecting the gains of the poorer segments of society at the expense of the middle-income groups in these two countries. Second, the share of the richest 10 per cent of the world's population has increased from 51.6 to 53.4 per cent of total world income (Bourguignon and Morrison, 2002). Third, when China and India are not factored into the analysis, available data show a rise in income inequality owing to the combined effect of higher income disparities within countries and the adverse distributive effect of faster population growth in poorer countries. Fourth, the income gap between the richest and poorest countries has widened in recent decades, as shown in figure III.2 (Berry and Serieux, 2002).

Table III.1 shows inequalities in the distribution of income among world regions, presenting the per capita income in each region as a percentage of per

Figure III.1. Evolution of income inequality among countries (*Gini coefficient values*)

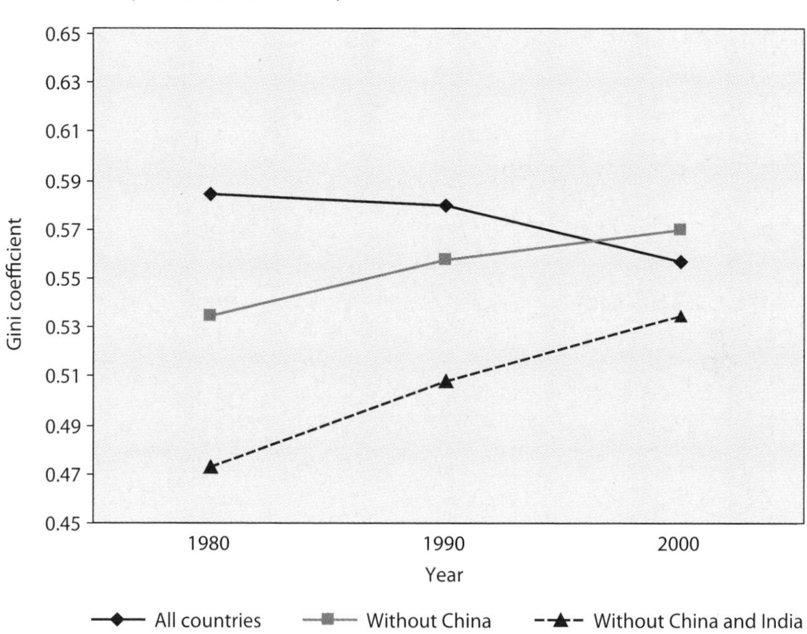

Source: A. Berry and J. Serieux, "Riding the elephants: the evolution of world economic growth and income distribution on the end of the 20th century" (unpublished paper).

Figure III.2. Per capita gross domestic product in the poorest and richest countries, 1960-1962 and 2000-2002 (*in constant 1995 US$, simple average*)

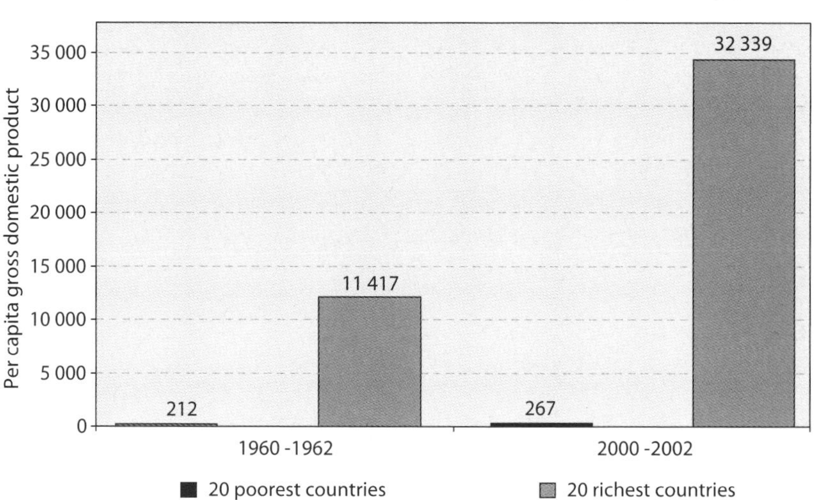

Source: World Commission on the Social Dimension of Globalization, *A Fair Globalization: Creating Opportunities for All* (Geneva, International Labour Organization, February 2004).

Table III.1. Regional per capita income as a share of high-income OECD countries' average per capita income[a] (*percentage*)

Region	*1980*	*1981-1985*	*1986-1990*	*1991-1995*	*1996-2000*	*2001*
Sub-Saharan Africa	3.3	3.1	2.5	2.1	2.0	1.9
South Asia	1.2	1.3	1.3	1.4	1.5	1.6
Middle East and North Africa	9.7	9.0	7.3	7.1	6.8	6.7
Latin America and the Caribbean	18.0	16.0	14.2	13.5	13.3	12.8
East Asia and the Pacific	1.5	1.7	1.9	2.5	3.1	3.3
High-income countries	97.7	97.6	97.6	97.9	97.9	97.8
High-income non-OECD countries	45.3	45.3	48.2	56.1	60.2	59.2
High-income OECD countries	100.0	100.0	100.0	100.0	100.0	100.0

Source: Alemayehu Geda, "Openness, inequality and poverty in Africa: exploring the role of global interdependence", paper presented at the workshop on regional studies of the International Forum for Social Development, held in New York on 17 and 18 June 2004.

[a] In constant United States dollars.

capita income in the rich OECD countries as a group, as well as the changes in these ratios over the past two decades. A review of the figures indicates that per capita income in all developing regions except South Asia and East Asia and the Pacific has declined relative to that in the high-income OECD countries.

Per capita income levels in sub-Saharan Africa, the Middle East and North Africa, and Latin America and the Caribbean have been steadily declining relative to the average per capita income in the wealthier OECD countries. Between 1980 and 2001 these levels decreased from 3.3 to 1.9 per cent in sub-Saharan Africa, from 9.7 to 6.7 per cent in the Middle East and North Africa, and from 18 to 12.8 per cent in Latin America and Caribbean. The decline in the ratios indicates not that per capita income in developing regions has decreased in absolute terms, but that per capita income has grown faster in the richer regions than in the poorer ones, widening the inequality gap.

The income gap between the wealthy OECD countries and the corresponding group of non-OECD countries[1] actually narrowed during the period under review; between 1980 and 2001 the per capita income of the latter as a proportion of the former rose from 45.3 to 59.2 per cent. Asia registered only moderate improvement relative to the high-income OECD countries, with ratios rising from 1.2 to 1.6 per cent in South Asia, and from 1.5 to 3.3 per cent in East Asia and the Pacific.

Income inequality within countries

Some studies contend that within individual countries there has been little or no change in income distribution or levels of income inequality in decades (Gustaffson and Johansson, 1999; Melchior, Telle and Wiig, 2000). An analysis of the information provided in the World Income Inequality Database (WIID) shows that within-country income inequality decreased during the 1950s, 1960s and 1970s in most developed, developing and centrally planned economies.[2] Since the 1980s, however, this decline has slowed or levelled off, and within many countries income inequality is rising once again (Cornia, 2004). Similar conclusions have been reached using different sets of data, which describe a significant increase in within-country income inequality over the past two decades (Atkinson, 2003; Harrison and Bluestone, 1988).

An analysis of WIID figures indicates that within-country income inequality rose between the 1950s and the 1990s in 48 of the 73 countries for which sufficiently reliable data are available (see table III.2). Together, these 48 countries account for 59 per cent of the combined population of the countries included in the analysis. In the early 1980s, 29 of the 73 countries had Gini coefficients[3] higher than 0.35-0.40, the threshold beyond which growth and poverty alleviation can be perceptibly affected; by the mid- to late 1990s, the number of countries with such high levels of income inequal-

Table III.2. Distribution of countries according to trends in Gini coefficients for income distribution between the 1950s and the 1990s (*sample of 73 developed, developing and transitional countries*)

		Sample countries' percentage share of:			
Trends in Gini coefficients	*Number of countries in group*	*Total population of sample countries*	*World population*	*GDP-PPP[a] of sample countries*	*World GDP-PPP[a]*
Rising	48	59	47	78	71
Continuously rising/ rising- stable	19	4	3	5	5
U-shaped	29	55	44	73	66
Falling	9	5	4	9	8
Continuously falling	6	3	3	7	7
Inverted U-shape	3	2	1	2	1
No trend	16	36	29	13	12
Not included in sample	–	–	20	–	9
Total	73	100	100	100	100

Source: G.A. Cornia, T. Addison and S. Kiiski, "Income distribution changes and their impact in the post-Second World War period", in *Inequality, Growth and Poverty in the Era of Liberalization and Globalization*, A.G. Cornia, ed. (Oxford, Oxford University Press/ United Nations University, World Institute for Economics Research, 2004).

[a] Gross domestic product - purchasing power parity.

ity had risen to 48. Within-country income inequality remained relatively constant in 16 of the countries under review, though the data suggest that the situation has worsened in three of them during the past few years. Only nine of the countries included in the analysis registered a decline in income inequality between the 1950s and the 1990s; included in this group are the Bahamas, France, Germany, Honduras, Jamaica, Malaysia, the Philippines, the Republic of Korea, and Tunisia (Cornia, Addison and Kiiski, 2004).

Within-country income inequality has risen in many developing countries and in a surprisingly large number of industrialized countries. Although data are not fully comparable across countries, a study of the evolution of income inequality in nine OECD countries generally supports the view that a significant shift has occurred in the distribution of income in all the countries analysed, with the possible exception of Canada. In some countries and country groupings, such as Finland and the United Kingdom of Great Britain and Northern Ireland, there have been increases of more than 10 Gini points in the past three decades. Empirical evidence from the study suggests that these figures have been influenced by technological change and the process of globalization, though it is acknowledged in the analysis that the distribution of income is a highly complex phenomenon, and that a single explanation does not suffice for all countries (Atkinson, 2003).

All of the former centrally planned economies of Europe and the former Soviet Union have experienced increases in within-country inequality. Among the transition countries of Central Europe, income concentration increased moderately throughout the 1990s, probably owing to the preservation of the welfare state system (Milanovic, 1998). In the countries of the former Soviet Union and south-eastern Europe, income inequality rose by an average of 10 to 20 Gini points, and the number of people living in poverty jumped from 14 million in 1989 to 147 million in 1996 (Cornia and Kiiski, 2001). The abrupt dismantling of the State-run welfare system after the collapse of the communist regimes in these countries played an important role in this dramatic increase.

A number of South and East Asian countries that were once able to achieve growth with equity have also experienced a sharp increase in income inequality in recent years. The Gini coefficient began rising in some of these countries in the late 1980s; however, in the 1990s rising inequality became a common feature in most. In some cases, the increase in income inequality appears to be closely related to a widening of the urban-rural income gap (Cornia, Addison and Kiiski, 2004).

Historically, the highest levels of income inequality have been found in Africa and Latin America, and in the 1980s and 1990s the situation deteriorated even further. An analysis by the Economic Commission for Latin America and the Caribbean (ECLAC) shows that, with few exceptions, the Gini coefficients for countries in the region between the 1950s and the beginning of the 1970s were among the highest in the world, ranging from 0.45 to 0.55 (Sainz, 2004). During the 1970s, income inequality declined moderately throughout the region, but a series of external shocks and the debt crises in the 1980s affected income distribution, and levels of income inequality rose again in most countries (Altimir, 1996). Those countries that had previously enjoyed a more equal distribution of income were the most profoundly affected by these developments. During the 1990s, income distribution trends deteriorated further, as reflected in the higher Gini coefficients in most countries.[4]

One feature that distinguishes patterns of within-country inequality in Latin America from those in other regions is the share of the richest 10 per cent of households in total income. In the 1990s these wealthier households accounted for more than 30 per cent of total income, with their share reaching 35 or even 45 per cent in some cases. By contrast, the poorest 40 per cent of households in Latin America garnered only 9 to 15 per cent of total income. By the end of the 1990s, the relative share of total income among the wealthiest 10 per cent of the population had increased in eight countries, declined somewhat in five, and held steady in one.

The largest income gap is in Brazil, where the per capita income of the most affluent 10 per cent of the population is 32 times that of the poorest 40 per cent. The lowest levels of income inequality in the region can be found in Uruguay and Costa Rica, countries in which the respective per capita income levels of the wealthiest 10 per cent are 8.8 and 12.6 times higher than those of the poorest 40 per cent. Although comparable figures are not available for the rest of the region, other indicators suggest that Cuba has probably maintained a less regressive income distribution than the other countries, despite the strong deterioration of its economy during the first half of the 1990s (Sainz, 2004).

The limited statistics for sub-Saharan Africa show that high levels of income inequality have persisted since the 1970s. Income inequality within rural areas has risen in countries that have high land concentration or are extremely dependent on the export of a single commodity, but has remained constant in countries such as Mozambique and Uganda, where small-scale agriculture is common (Bigsten, 2000).

In many countries, especially developing countries, the rise in income inequality at the national level is strongly correlated with increases in rural-urban and regional income inequality. According to an analysis of data from several Asian countries, the rural-urban income gap rose rapidly in China, India and Thailand during the 1990s. In the case of China, half of the overall increase in income inequality since 1985 is attributable to differences in income distribution among the country's various regions. Similar trends have been observed for Thailand and, more recently, for India (Cornia and Kiiski, 2001). Conversely, data from Latin America show that the income gap between rural and urban areas has been narrowing.

Poverty

The negative trends in income distribution imply that monetary poverty has gradually worsened in many parts of the world. As the seriousness of the problem has grown more evident, poverty and poverty reduction strategies have become increasingly prominent in the development discourse. Since the World Summit for Social Development, Governments have intensified their efforts to address poverty, setting national poverty reduction targets and formulating and implementing plans and strategies for poverty eradication. Anti-poverty programmes have focused not only on monetary issues, but also on improving access to basic social services such as health and education, especially for vulnerable groups; promoting employment opportunities; providing social protection; and applying measures to address the adverse effects of financial crises.

At the global level considerable progress has been made in reducing poverty over the past two decades, largely as a result of the more focused anti-poverty programmes and policies. Table III.3 indicates that the proportion of the world's population living in extreme or absolute poverty (surviving on less than US$ 1 a day) declined noticeably between 1981 and 2001, dropping from 40 to 21 per cent. At the regional level, only East Asia and the Pacific, the Middle East and North Africa, and South Asia registered sharp declines during this period.

Overall poverty reduction statistics mask wide national and regional differences and the uneven pace of progress. The advances made in China and India have contributed substantially to the positive picture at the global level. Because these two countries account for 38 per cent of the world's population, the rapid expansion of their respective economies has led to a significant reduction in the number of people living in absolute poverty worldwide; between 1990 and 2000 this figure declined from 1.2 billion to 1.1 billion (International Labour Organization, 2004). In China alone, the proportion of people living on less than US$ 2 a day fell from 88 to 47 per cent between 1981 and 2001, and the number of people living on less than US$ 1 per day was reduced from 634 million to 212 million. In India, the proportion living on less than US$ 2 per day declined from 90 to 80 per cent, and the number living in extreme poverty decreased slightly, from 382 million to 359 million.

The improvements in China and India notwithstanding, in 2001 more than 1.1 billion people worldwide were struggling to survive on less than US$ 1 a day. Poverty is more prevalent and persistent in certain regions. In sub-Saharan Africa, for example, the number of poor people increased by almost 90 million in a little more than a decade (1990-2001). Even in regions that have achieved significant progress, such as South and East Asia, rates of poverty reduction have been, at best, uneven.

In Europe and Central Asia the total number of people living on less than US$ 1 a day grew by more than 14 million between 1981 and 2001. The incidence of poverty in these regions increased sharply in the 1990s, but by 2001 the upward trend had slowed. Worsening poverty in Eastern Europe and the Commonwealth of Independent States (CIS) has contributed substantially to the trend towards increased poverty in Europe and Central Asia since 1993. By the end of the 1990s, 50 million people were living in poor families in the former socialist countries, and the same was true for 43 million people in the CIS (United Nations Children's Fund, 2001). During the 1990s, poverty and income inequality rose steadily in the Central Asian Republics. In Tajikistan, a 14 per cent increase in the country's population was accompanied by a 64 per cent decline in GDP and escalating poverty levels. In Azerbaijan, sound macroeconomic policies have ensured economic stability and high real GDP growth; however, these economic successes have not been reflected in the lives of people, 49 per cent of whom live in poverty. In 2002, about half of the population in Kyrgyzstan lived below the poverty line (United Nations Development Programme, 2004a).

In Latin America and the Caribbean the proportion of those living on less than US$ 1 a day fell slightly overall, declining from 11.3 to 9.5 per cent between 1990 and 2001, though poverty levels increased in many individual countries during this period. The most important exception is Chile, where poverty declined sharply in the 1990s. Rates of poverty and unemployment rose to record highs in Argentina, but the country has enjoyed steady eco-

Table III.3. Poverty rates for the world, major regions, and China and India

	Poverty rate (percentage living on less than US$ 1 per day)							
Region/country	*1981*	*1984*	*1987*	*1990*	*1993*	*1996*	*1999*	*2001*
World	40	33	28	28	26	23	22	21
East Asia and the Pacific	58	39	28	30	25	17	16	15
Europe and Central Asia	1	1	0	1	4	4	6	4
Latin America and the Caribbean	10	12	11	11	11	11	11	10
Middle East and North Africa	5	4	3	2	2	2	3	2
South Asia	52	47	45	41	40	37	32	31
Sub-Saharan Africa	42	46	47	45	44	46	46	47
China	64	41	29	33	28	17	18	17
India	54	50	46	42	42	42	35	35

	Poverty rate (percentage living on less than US$ 2 per day)							
Region/country	*1981*	*1984*	*1987*	*1990*	*1993*	*1996*	*1999*	*2001*
World	67	64	60	61	60	56	54	53
East Asia and the Pacific	85	77	68	70	65	53	50	47
Europe and Central Asia	5	4	3	5	17	21	24	20
Latin America and the Caribbean	27	30	28	28	30	24	25	25
Middle East and North Africa	29	25	24	21	20	22	24	23
South Asia	89	87	87	86	85	82	78	77
Sub-Saharan Africa	73	76	76	75	75	75	76	77
China	88	79	67	73	68	53	50	47
India	90	88	87	86	86	85	81	80

Region/country	*Number of people living on less than US$ 1 per day (in millions)*							
	1981	*1984*	*1987*	*1990*	*1993*	*1996*	*1999*	*2001*
World	2 450	2 480	2 478	2 654	2 764	2 674	2 739	2 735
East Asia and the Pacific	1 170	1 109	1 028	1 116	1 079	922	900	864
Europe and Central Asia	20	18	15	23	81	98	113	93
Latin America and the Caribbean	99	119	115	125	136	117	127	128
Middle East and North Africa	52	50	53	51	52	61	70	70
South Asia	821	859	911	958	1 005	1 029	1 039	1 064
Sub-Saharan Africa	288	326	355	382	410	447	489	516
China	876	814	731	825	803	650	627	594
India	630	662	697	731	770	807	805	826

Source: World Bank Poverty Monitor (http://www.worldbank.org/research/povmonitor; accessed 7 February 2005).

nomic growth since 2003. This economic expansion has not led to a more balanced distribution of wealth or a reduction in social inequalities, however. For example, in 1994 the income of the richest 10 per cent of the population was nearly 20 times that of the poorest 10 per cent; by 2004 the ratio was 29 to 1 (South-North Development Monitor, 2005).

While the proportion of the world's population living on less than US$ 1 a day decreased significantly between 1981 and 2001 (from 40 to 21 per cent), the share of those living on less than US$ 2 a day declined less dramatically (from 67 to 53 per cent). In East Asia and the Pacific only 15 per cent of the population was living on less than US$ 1 a day in 2001, but the proportion living on less than US$ 2 a day was close to 50 per cent. Despite China's remarkable economic progress and its influence on global trends, 47 per cent of the population was living on less than US$ 2 a day in 2001 (see table III.3). The slower decline in the proportion of those living on less than US$ 2 a day reflects the fact that a sizeable number of people have moved from the lowest poverty category into this marginally better income category. The combination of the transfer between poverty categories and various demographic and economic developments has resulted in a global increase in the number of people living in poverty (those living on less than US$ 2 per day) since the late 1990s (Chen and Ravallion, 2000).

Perhaps even more important than the increasing levels of poverty is the emergence and entrenchment of new patterns of poverty in a number of countries. Developments worth noting include an increased tendency for people to rotate in and out of poverty, a rise in urban poverty and stagnation in rural poverty, and increases in the proportion of informal workers among the urban poor and in the number of unemployed poor.

The tendency for individuals to move in and out of poverty has grown since the 1980s, illustrating how the path out of poverty is often not linear. This phenomenon can lead to some of the worst forms of social exclusion because those who are not classified as poor in a particular period may be overlooked by social assistance programmes. In many African countries around a quarter of the population may be deemed consistently poor; however, up to an additional 60 per cent move in and out of poverty (Economic Commission for Africa, 2003). In Latin America, fluctuations in employment and income account for an increasing share of the population cycling in and out of poverty. In the Russian Federation, nearly half of the households deemed very poor in 1992 were not classified as such a year later, demonstrating that the poor do not constitute a static group. Indeed, some households rose above the poverty level in 1992/93, even as overall poverty levels were increasing (World Bank, 1995).

The increasing urbanization of poverty and the lack of notable progress in ameliorating well-entrenched rural poverty present new challenges to development. Poverty has traditionally been viewed as a primarily rural phenomenon, and the depth of poverty remains greater in rural areas; however, a growing number of urban areas are experiencing serious levels of poverty as well. In Latin America, poverty is more prevalent in urban areas. In 1999, for example, only 77 million of the region's 211 million poor lived in rural areas, while the remaining 134 million lived in urban areas. Nevertheless, the concentration of poverty was still much greater in rural areas, with the poor accounting for 64 per cent of the rural population but only 37 per cent of the urban population. Poverty in rural areas is also more extreme (Sainz, 2004).

In Africa, where the worst forms of poverty exist, an estimated 59 per cent of the rural population live in extreme poverty, compared with 43 per cent of the urban population. Among the factors undermining poverty reduction efforts in the region are high rates of population growth; the high prevalence of unskilled labour; and the HIV/AIDS epidemic, which has seriously reduced the overall calibre of the workforce. The net effect of these circumstances is that per capita income in the region did not change between 1990 and 1999 even though aggregate GDP increased by 29 per cent.

In many countries, the lack of sufficient and sustained income growth has been a major obstacle to reducing poverty. Among the 155 developing and transition countries for which data are available, only 30 achieved annual per capita income growth of at least 3 per cent during the 1990s, while 71 registered rates of less than 3 per cent; a total of 54 countries (including 20 in sub-Saharan Africa) experienced a decline in per capita income in this period (United Nations Development Programme, 2003).

Demographic trends have led many households, communities and countries deeper into poverty. High fertility increases poverty by diverting household resources from savings to consumption. It also makes government investment in education and other forms of human capital formation more difficult, as more and more resources have to be allocated to meet the needs of a rapidly growing population. Persistently high fertility produces elevated age dependency ratios, indicating a high proportion of the young (0-14 years) and the old (65 years or above) relative to those in the prime working-age group. Greater dependence places increased pressure on the earnings of a limited workforce in a way that perpetuates poverty even among those who are employed. Internal and international migration are strongly linked to poverty as well; sending communities become poorer, as they tend to lose their most economically active members, and in receiving communities migrants are likely to be poorly integrated and without access to decent employment and are therefore vulnerable to extreme poverty.

Unemployment

Of all the inequalities within and between countries, the inability of an increasing share of the world's job-seeking population to secure employment has perhaps the most far-reaching implications. Most of those looking for work are adults with personal and household responsibilities. People who cannot secure adequate employment are unable to generate an income sufficient to cover their health, education and other basic needs and those of their families, or to accumulate savings to protect their households from the vicissitudes of the economy. The unemployed are among the most vulnerable in society and are therefore more likely to suffer from poverty in all its manifestations.

A fundamental component of any successful development strategy is an employment strategy that not only addresses the creation of decent jobs but also promotes adequate working conditions in which freedom, equality, security and dignity figure prominently (United Nations, 2004c). The Programme of Action of the World Summit for Social Development states that "productive work and employment are central elements of development as well as decisive elements of human identity" (United Nations, 1995, para. 42). It has been 10 years since full employment was identified as a core objective; however, the progress that has been achieved falls far short of expectations. The Summit participants were hopeful that significant strides could be made towards ensuring freely chosen productive employment and work for all; instead, global unemployment levels have risen in the past decade.

It is estimated that between 1993 and 2003 the number of unemployed rose from 140 million to an unprecedented 186 million, representing 6.2 per cent of the total working population (International Labour Organization, 2005c). By the end of this period the ranks of the working poor had swelled to 550 million. In developed countries as a group, the unemployment rate fell from around 8 per cent in 1993 to 6.8 per cent in 2003 (see table III.4), while much of the developing world experienced stagnating or rising unemployment during this time. The world regions with the lowest and highest

Table III.4. Unemployment rates, labour force growth rates and GDP growth rates for the world and major regions

	Unemployment rate			*Annual labour force growth rate*	*Annual GDP growth rate*
Region/country grouping	*1993*	*2002*	*2003*	*1993-2003*	*1993-2003*
World	5.6	6.3	6.2	1.8	3.5
Industrialized economies	8.0	6.8	6.8	0.8	2.5
Transition economies	6.3	9.4	9.2	−0.1	0.2
East Asia	2.4	3.1	3.3	1.3	8.3
Latin America and the Caribbean	6.9	9.0	8.0	2.3	2.6
Middle East and North Africa	12.1	11.9	12.2	3.3	3.5
South Asia	4.8	4.8	4.8	2.3	5.5
South-East Asia	3.9	7.1	6.3	2.4	4.4
Sub-Saharan Africa	11.0	10.8	10.9	2.8	2.9

Source: International Labour Organization, "Global trends in employment, productivity and poverty, 2005" (http://www.ilo.org/public/english/employment/strat/download/wr04c1en.pdf; accessed 17 February 2005).

levels of unemployment, which remained relatively stable during the decade under review, were East Asia (around 3 per cent) and the Middle East and North Africa (12.2 per cent).

Between 1993 and 2003 unemployment increased by as much as 62 per cent in some parts of South-East Asia and Latin America and the Caribbean. Although the overall level of unemployment rose in East Asia, it remained well below that found in other regions. South-East Asia registered the most substantial increase in unemployment during the period under review, largely owing to the high annual labour force growth rate of 2.4 per cent and the fact that some of the countries in the region, including Indonesia (the largest), were slow to recover from the Asian financial crisis of 1997/98. The data indicate that unemployment decreased slightly in South-East Asia and Latin America and the Caribbean between 2002 and 2003, though it should be noted that the changes were relatively small, occurred over a single year, and may reflect only a temporary or cyclical decline.

In sub-Saharan Africa, the labour force grew by 2.8 per cent annually and unemployment declined only slightly between 1993 and 2003, leaving the overall unemployment rate virtually unchanged. In the transition economies unemployment rose by 46 per cent during this period.

Among the countries for which reliable data are available, half have reported a decrease and the other half an increase in unemployment rates since 1995 (International Labour Organization, 2005a). Trends have varied from one region to another. In Latin America and the Caribbean, overall unemployment has been rising since the 1990s despite the stagnant unemployment situation in Brazil and the decline in unemployment in Mexico (Economic Commission for Latin America and the Caribbean, 2005a). Almost all East Asian and South-East Asian countries have experienced rising unemployment during the past decade as well.

Before 1980, employment in China was growing steadily at about 2.6 per cent, but the rate dropped to 1.1 per cent in the 1990s. India also experienced a significant decline in employment growth in the 1990s, reflecting a slowdown in both rural and urban areas. Between 1993 and 2000 growth in rural employment fell to 0.67 per cent, the lowest rate in the country's post-independence history. Nonetheless, the unemployment rate in India rose only slightly, whereas the corresponding rates for Bangladesh and Pakistan increased noticeably.

Comparable trend data are not available for most sub-Saharan African countries. However, the extremely high levels of unemployment in the region are worth noting; in 1999, Botswana, Burkina Faso, Niger, South Africa and Tanzania all had unemployment rates of 20 per cent or higher.

It is important to bear in mind that the unemployment rate alone is not a clear indicator of the extent of equality or inequality in the labour force. Beneath the tip of this iceberg are a number of other employment-related factors that may exacerbate or ameliorate inequalities, including the size and growth of the informal economy, the quality of work and wage levels (see chapter II). The fact is that most of the poor in developing countries are not unemployed. They work but cannot earn enough to raise themselves and their families above the poverty threshold. Further, as mentioned previously, many are subject to exploitation and lack basic rights and protections in the workplace.

Recognizing the critical importance of these issues, the ILO has come up with a "decent work" agenda that constitutes an integral part of the overall United Nations development agenda. The overarching objective of the decent work agenda is to promote opportunities for women and men to obtain decent and productive work under conditions of freedom, equality, security and human dignity. The agenda encompasses the following four strategic objectives: (*a*) the opportunity to be employed doing work that is productive and is fairly remunerated; (*b*) security in the workplace and social protection for workers and their families; (*c*) freedom of expression, organization, and participation in activities affecting the lives of workers; and (*d*) equal opportunities for men and women (International Labour Organization, 2005b). Labour market access and employment are considered vital for social inclusion. The ILO is working to protect the rights of all workers and has identified meaningful employment as essential in both eradicating poverty and helping people to fulfil their human potential (International Labour Organization, 2004). The decent work agenda addresses a number of challenges that have arisen from globalization, including the loss of employment, the inequitable distribution of benefits, and the disruption that has been caused in so many people's lives. Answering these challenges will require the participation of actors at all levels.

Non-economic aspects of inequality

As noted previously, the traditional focus on economic inequality is directed almost exclusively towards income differentials within and between countries, while the social underpinnings are neglected. It is not possible to assess or address inequality until the importance and interconnectedness of its economic and non-economic aspects are widely acknowledged. Non-economic indicators relating to priorities such as health, education, access to basic necessities (food, water, sanitation and housing) and opportunities for political participation are closely linked to individual, household and national economic status. Countries that have the poorest education and health profiles are generally at the bottom of the economic development ladder. The present section summarizes patterns and trends relating to selected aspects of non-economic inequality, including health, hunger and malnutrition, and education. An effort is made to demonstrate how differentials in these areas are linked to some of the economic inequalities that tend to dominate discussions of global inequality.

Health

Significant advances have been made in recent years in the field of health. The health status of many has improved as a result of this progress, but inequalities within and between countries have worsened because the benefits of better health have not accrued evenly. The more privileged segments of the population, by virtue of their better education, income, geographical location or political clout, are often better able to harness the benefits deriving from advances in health. Developing countries are at a distinct disadvantage, as they typically have less access to advanced diagnostic technologies that contribute to the identification and treatment of diseases at advanced stages, to therapeutic remedies such as antiretroviral treatments for HIV and AIDS, and to medicines for preventing or treating endemic diseases such as malaria. Since poverty can contribute to ill health, and poor health can in turn perpetuate poverty, poorer people and countries are often caught in a vicious cycle that deepens their deprivation in relation to non-poor groups.

Health-related inequalities, including differentials in access to health services, have perhaps become the most frequently cited indicators of non-economic inequality. Discussions of causes, effects and possible solutions have been a central feature of the development debate in the international arena, and health figures prominently in the Millennium Development Goals. Within countries, reducing disparities in health and mortality between socio-economic groups, between urban and rural areas, and between regions has been a priority concern of Governments.

Over the past 50 years or so, global efforts to improve health and life expectancy have met with considerable success. Infant and child health has improved, and child mortality rates have declined. More women have gained access to safe and effective contraception, which prevents many unwanted pregnancies and reduces maternal mortality resulting from unsafe abortions. Global health statistics are indicative of enormous progress in these and other areas, but they conceal the wide variability within and between countries and regions. They also obscure the fact that, as a result of asymmetries in globalization, the health benefits accruing to poorer individuals and countries represent a tiny fraction of the benefits made possible by major technological and scientific advances. The inequality predicament is evident regardless of how health status is measured.

Life expectancy

Worldwide, life expectancy has increased from about 47 to 65 years over the past five decades. However, statistics show a gap of up to 36 years between the regions with the lowest and highest life expectancies (see figure III.3). Since 1990-1995, Australia/New Zealand has had the highest life expectancy of 77-79 years; the corresponding figures for other world regions have been either slightly or significantly lower.

Figure III.3. Inequalities in life expectancy between major world regions: deviations of regional life expectancy at birth from that of Australia/New Zealand (1990-1995 and 2000-2005)

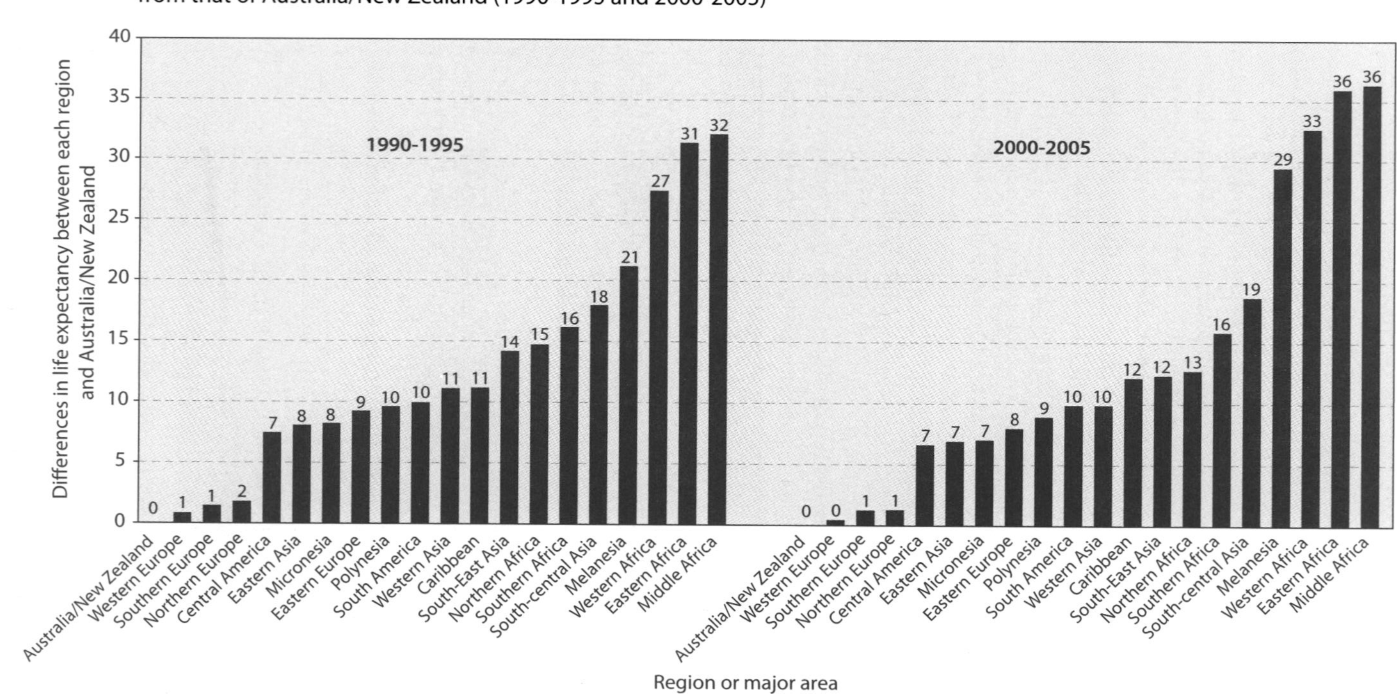

Source: Based on data from *World Population Prospects: The 2002 Revision* (United Nations publication, Sales No. E.03.XIII.8).

Figure III.4. Distribution of all countries according to how far their life expectancy falls below that of Japan, 1990 and 2000

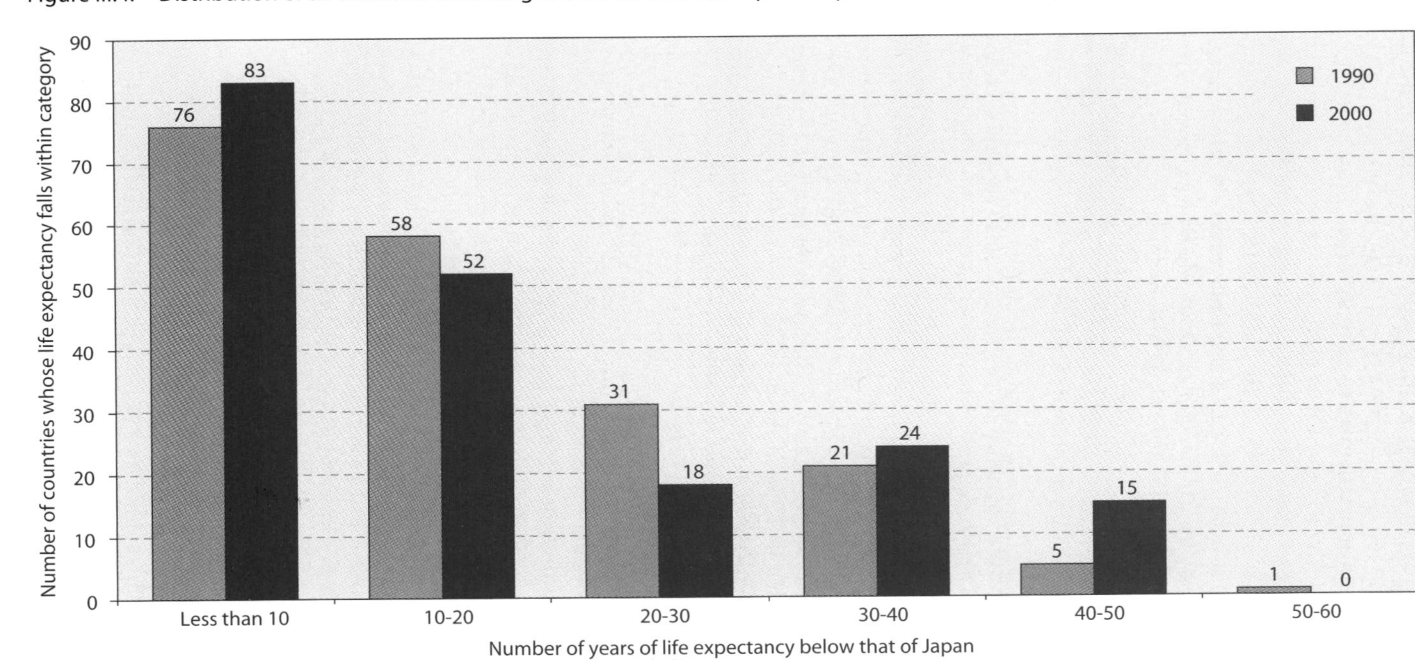

Source: Based on data from *World Population Prospects: The 2002 Revision* (United Nations publication, Sales No. E.03.XII.8).

When inequalities in life expectancy are assessed in terms of the number of regions falling more than 25 years short of the region with the highest life expectancy, it is apparent that the situation has worsened since 1990. In 1990-1995 and 1995-2000, the central, eastern and western regions of Africa were the only regions with life expectancy more than 25 years below that of Australia/New Zealand. By 2000-2005, largely as a result of the AIDS epidemic, southern Africa had been placed in the same category. It is worth noting that by 2000-2005 differentials had narrowed somewhat in the regions with higher longevity and also in those with lower longevity, suggesting increasing polarization between the two groups. Life expectancy differentials among the four worst-performing regions have narrowed in particular, even as their performance in relation to the rest of the world has worsened.

Country-level differentials in life expectancy also suggest increased polarization between the best and worst performers. Figure III.4 shows the distribution of all countries according to how far their life expectancy for 1990-1995 and 2000-2005 fell short of that of Japan, which had the highest life expectancy for both periods. There were many more countries that fell within 10 years of Japan's life expectancy in 2000-2005 than in 1995-2000, suggesting a degree of improvement in the level of inequality. However, there was also a substantial increase in the number of countries with life expectancies 30 to 50 years short of Japan's (the worst performers). The number of countries in the middle category (with life expectancies 20 to 30 years short of Japan's) declined by almost half, largely because Haiti and 12 sub-Saharan African countries experienced a regression.

This pattern is consistent with the notion of "club convergence", in which poor countries tend to have lower average life expectancy while richer countries converge towards a higher level (Mayer-Foulkes, 2001). It is also consistent with the conclusion from recent analysis that inequality in the distribution of health gains has increased (Cornia and Menchini, 2005).

An important aspect of inequalities in life expectancy is the male-female longevity gap. Almost everywhere, life expectancy is higher for females than for males. Underlying this disparity, which is most pronounced in Eastern Europe, are a number of factors associated with lifestyle, including the higher exposure of males to health and mortality risks linked to certain occupations, motor vehicle accidents, and the excessive use of tobacco and alcohol.

Maternal and child health

Child mortality declined between 1990 and 2001, though somewhat more slowly in developing countries. Widespread immunization against killer childhood diseases has contributed significantly to reducing infant and child mortality; over a period of several decades enormously successful vaccination policies and programmes have been implemented in many countries with the

Table III.5. Levels of under-five mortality for selected countries and between-country inequality indices

Region/country	*Year*	*Under-five mortality (5q0) per 1 000 births*	*Inequality index*[a]
Sub-Saharan Africa			
Gabon	2000	88.6	–
Zimbabwe	1999	102.1	13.5
Nigeria	1999	140.1	51.5
Tanzania	2000/2001	146.6	58.0
Uganda	2000/2001	151.5	62.9
Benin	2001	160.0	71.4
Ethiopia	2000	166.2	77.6
Zambia	2001/2002	168.2	79.6
Guinea	1999	176.9	88.3
Malawi	2000	188.6	100.0
Rwanda	1999	196.2	107.6
Burkina Faso	1998/1999	219.1	130.5
Mali	2001	229.1	140.5
North Africa/West Asia/Europe			
Armenia	2000	39.0	–
Egypt	2000	54.3	15.3
Central Asia			
Kazakhstan	1999	71.4	–
Turkmenistan	2000	94.3	22.9
South and South-East Asia			
Nepal	2001	91.2	–
Bangladesh	1999/2000	94.1	2.9
India	1998/1999	94.9	3.7
Cambodia	2000	124.4	33.2
Latin America and the Caribbean			
Colombia	2000	24.9	–
Dominican Republic	1999	30.4	5.5
Peru	2000	46.7	21.8
Guatemala	1998/1999	58.7	33.8
Haiti	2000	118.6	93.7

Source: Under-five mortality data obtained from ORC Macro, MEASURE DHS STATcompiler (http://www.measuredhs.com; accessed 15 February 2005).

[a] The inequality index is calculated as the value of 5q0 for the selected country minus the value for the country with the lowest 5q0 within that region.

assistance of United Nations entities such as the United Nations Children's Fund (UNICEF) and the World Health Organization (WHO). Since 1974 the proportion of children under the age of one who are immunized against diphtheria, polio, tetanus, measles, tuberculosis (TB) and pertussis (whooping cough) has risen from 5 per cent to nearly 75 per cent.

These positive trends are apparent at the global level but do not reveal the stagnation and even worsening of the child health and mortality situation in certain parts of the world. Since the beginning of the 1990s, for example, global inequalities have widened as mortality among newborns has risen in sub-Saharan Africa but declined in most other regions (World Health Or-

Table III.6. Under-five mortality for countries with the highest and lowest rates, 1995, 2000 and 2002

	Under-five mortality (per 1 000 births)				Under-five mortality (per 1 000 births)		
Countries with the highest mortality[a]	*1995*	*2000*	*2002*	*Countries with the lowest mortality*[a]	*1995*	*2000*	*2002*
Central African Republic	180	180	180	Sweden	4	4	3
Malawi	216	188	182	Denmark	7	5	4
Zambia	182	182	182	Iceland	5	4	4
Mauritania	183	183	183	Norway	6	4	4
Burundi	190	190	190	Singapore	5	4	4
Côte d'Ivoire	175	188	191	Austria	7	5	5
Chad	200	200	200	Czech Republic	8	5	5
Nigeria	238	205	201	Finland	4	5	5
Rwanda	209	203	203	Germany	7	5	5
Democratic Republic of the Congo	205	205	205	Greece	9	6	5
Mozambique	221	208	205	Japan	6	5	5
Burkina Faso	207	207	207	Republic of Korea	6	5	5
Guinea-Bissau	235	215	211	Luxembourg	6	5	5
Mali	233	224	222	Malta	11	6	5
Somalia	225	225	225	Monaco	5	5	5
Liberia	235	235	235	Netherlands	6	6	5
Afghanistan	257	257	257	Slovenia	7	5	5
Angola	260	260	260	Australia	6	6	6
Niger	295	270	264	Belgium	9	6	6
Sierra Leone	293	286	284	Brunei Darussalam	9	7	6

Source: United Nations Statistics Division, Millennium Indicators Database (http://millenniumindicators.un.org/unsd/).
[a] Ranked according to the level of under-five mortality in 2002.

ganization, 2005b). This increase may be partly attributable to the high risk of mortality among the children of HIV-positive mothers, but poverty and health policies that deny the poor access to health services play a major role as well.

Between-country disparities in under-five mortality are large and persistent, despite increased attention and intervention over the past 50 years. Data for selected countries indicate that under-five mortality rates in 2000 ranged from 25 per 1,000 live births in Colombia to 229 per 1,000 live births in Mali (see table III.5). Exceptionally high rates (more than 100 deaths per 1,000 live births) are evident for almost all of sub-Saharan Africa and for Cambodia and Haiti. The 20 countries with the highest rates and the 20 countries with the lowest rates in the world in 2002 are shown in table III.6, along with their respective under-five mortality levels for 1995, 2000 and 2002. The data clearly indicate that the best-performing countries suffer virtually no under-five mortality, while in most of the worst-performing countries more than one in five children die before they reach the age of five. Of the 20 countries with the highest rates, 19 are in sub-Saharan Africa, the region that experienced the smallest decline (from 186 to 174 deaths per 1,000 live births, or a reduction of only 2 per cent) between 1990 and 2001.

Large differentials in under-five mortality can also be found within most countries. Data from recent Demographic and Health Surveys (DHS) indicate that rates are consistently higher in rural areas than in urban areas (ORC Macro, 2005). The data show that in countries such as Armenia (2000), Brazil (1996), Burkina Faso (1998/99), Colombia (2000), Côte d'Ivoire (1998/99), Egypt (1995), Ghana (1998), Nicaragua (2001) and Peru (2002), rural rates have been at least 1.5 times higher than urban rates of under-five mortality.

Among all the health indicators, maternal mortality rates reflect some of the greatest disparities between developed and developing countries. Ninety-nine per cent of maternal deaths worldwide occur in developing countries, and in poor countries as many as 30 per cent of deaths among women of reproductive age (15-49 years) may be from pregnancy-related causes, compared with rates of less than 1 per cent for developed countries. In 2000, there were 400 maternal deaths per 100,000 live births in developing regions, a ratio 19 times higher than in developed regions. The lifetime risk of maternal death was 1 in 61 for developing countries, which was 45 times greater than the risk of 1 in 2,800 for developed countries. Even among developing countries, maternal mortality rates varied widely. Disparities were extreme at the regional level; in 2000, the lifetime risk of 1 in 16 for sub-Saharan Africa was 249 times greater than the risk of 1 in 4,000 for Western Europe. Equally disquieting is the extent of morbidity or illness women experience in connection with pregnancy and childbirth. Even when they survive childbirth, women who receive inadequate maternity care often suffer from the long-term effects of complications such as obstetric fistula, infection or prolonged anaemia from excessive blood loss during delivery.

Table III.7. Immunization coverage among children aged 12-23 months, by country and selected background characteristics

Country	Year	*Type of residence*		*Difference (urban minus rural)*	*Highest level of education*			*Difference (secondary and higher minus no education)*
		Urban	*Rural*		*No education*	*Primary education*	*Secondary education or higher*	
Armenia	2000	73.2	69.1	4.1	–	–	71.6	–
Bangladesh	1999/2000	69.6	58.6	11.0	53.8	60.1	72.5	18.7
Benin	2001	64.4	56.1	8.3	55.7	63.1	75.1	19.4
Burkina Faso	1998/1999	59.5	25.9	33.6	25.7	59.6	63.3	37.6
Cambodia	2000	46.3	39.0	7.3	29.1	41.4	58.8	29.7
Colombia	2000	54.8	46.0	8.8	26.7	46.9	56.6	29.9
Dominican Republic	1999	30.5	39.6	–9.1	–	29.9	40.3	–
Egypt	2000	92.8	91.8	1.0	91.4	92.9	92.6	1.2
Ethiopia	2000	42.0	11.0	31.0	10.2	24.8	45.0	34.8
Gabon	2000	17.8	5.7	12.1	19.3	10.2	17.3	-2.0
Guatemala	1998/1999	55.2	62.1	–6.9	52.4	62.1	64.4	12.0
Guinea	1999	47.3	26.7	20.6	29.7	39.1	53.9	24.2
Haiti	2000	33.6	33.5	0.1	23.2	37.7	43.6	20.4
India	1998/99	54.8	34.9	19.9	24.7	46.0	61.4	36.7
Kazakhstan	1999	74.9	71.7	3.2	–	–	73.1	–
Malawi	2000	78.6	68.7	9.9	64.0	70.8	87.5	23.5
Mali	2001	50.3	21.5	28.8	25.1	38.8	62.7	37.6
Mauritania	2000/2001	38.0	27.4	10.6	27.4	39.6	30.5	3.1
Nepal	2001	74.9	65.0	9.9	57.0	83.2	90.0	33.0
Nigeria	1999	31.7	11.3	20.4	6.3	18.1	36.1	29.8
Peru	2000	60.4	51.1	9.3	43.8	51.7	61.1	17.3
Rwanda	2000	77.0	75.8	1.2	72.2	76.8	82.1	9.9
Tanzania	1999	80.5	65.5	15.0	49.5	75.1	72.2	22.7
Turkmenistan	2000	80.1	88.5	–8.4	74.1	100.0	84.9	10.8
Uganda	2001/2002	42.1	36.0	6.1	28.3	37.2	51.1	22.8
Zambia	1999	76.9	67.2	9.7	58.0	70.6	76.3	18.3
Zimbabwe	1999	65.0	63.6	1.4	62.9	60.9	67.2	4.3

Source: ORC Macro, MEASURE DHS STATcompiler (http://www.measuredhs.com; accessed 15 February 2005).

Table III.8. Differentials within and between selected countries in access to skilled medical care at delivery for children born three years before the survey

		Assistance at delivery			
		Doctor or health professional		*No birth attendant*	
Country	*Year of survey*	*Urban*	*Rural*	*Urban*	*Rural*
Guatemala	1998/1999	67.2	26.1	–	2.0
Guinea	1999	77.1	21.8	2.5	9.0
Haiti	2000	54.2	12.0	2.8	4.5
India	1998/1999	73.3	33.5	0.1	0.6
Kazakhstan	1999	99.1	99.5	–	–
Malawi	2000	81.1	50.5	1.3	2.6
Mali	2001	81.7	27.4	5.4	19.1
Mauritania	2000/2001	85.9	29.1	1.6	10.9
Nepal	2001	53.7	11.5	4.0	8.4
Nigeria	1999	57.9	35.3	9.6	12.1
Peru	2000	86.5	27.4	0.4	1.7
Rwanda	2000	64.8	18.2	5.5	22.4
Tanzania	1999	82.7	33.5	1.0	8.7
Turkmenistan	2000	98.4	96.7	0.2	0.1
Uganda	2000/2001	81.3	33.4	4.4	15.5
Zambia	2001/2002	78.1	27.1	2.8	8.2
Zimbabwe	1999	90.0	64.3	1.0	4.4

Source: ORC Macro, MEASURE DHS STATcompiler (http://www.measuredhs.com; accessed 17 February 2005).

Health-related inequalities within and between countries are often the result of differentials in underlying determinants of health, including education, access to health services, sanitation and nutrition. For example, child mortality differentials are governed by disparities in proximate determinants such as access to skilled medical care, nutrition, immunization and education.

Although it is known that the immunization of all children against killer childhood diseases significantly reduces child mortality, differentials in immunization status remain wide both within and between countries. Table III.7 shows that within countries, immunization coverage is generally higher in urban areas and among children with more highly educated mothers. Between countries, urban disparities and rural disparities are sizeable. For example, urban coverage is under 50 per cent in Cambodia, the Dominican Republic, Ethiopia, Gabon, Guinea, Haiti, Mauritania, Nigeria and Uganda but over 80 per cent in Tanzania and Turkmenistan and 93 per cent in Egypt. Similarly, rural coverage remains below 20 per cent in Ethiopia, Gabon and Nigeria but around 90 per cent in Egypt and Turkmenistan. Inequalities are also evident across maternal education categories; women with little or no education are less likely to have their children immunized than are those with secondary or higher education. From a policy perspective, it is disconcerting that the high inequalities in infant and child mortality persist, given that rela-

Table III.9. Adults and children affected by HIV/AIDS: the world and major regions, 2004

Regions	*Adults and children living with HIV*	*Adults and children newly infected with HIV*	*Adult HIV prevalence (percentage)*	*Adult and child deaths due to AIDS*
World	39.4 million	4.9 million	1.1	3.1 million
Sub-Saharan Africa	25.4 million	3.1 million	7.4	2.3 million
North Africa and Middle East	0.54 million	92 000	0.3	28 000
East Asia	1.1 million	290 000	0.1	51 000
South and South-East Asia	7.1 million	890 000	0.6	490 000
Latin America	1.7 million	240 000	0.6	95 000
Caribbean	440 000	53 000	2.3	36 000
Eastern Europe and Central Asia	1.4 million	210 000	0.8	60 000
Western and Central Europe	0.61 million	21 000	0.3	6 500
North America	1.0 million	44 000	0.6	16 000

Source: UNAIDS, *AIDS Epidemic Update, December 2004* (http://www.unaids.org/wad2004/report.html; accessed 13 April 2005).

tively inexpensive preventive and remedial measures such as immunization against measles and other childhood diseases, the protection of drinking water, the practice of basic hygiene, and increased reliance on oral rehydration therapy and breastfeeding could prevent millions of deaths among children under the age of five every year. With regard to immunization, it is surprising that significant within-country differentials remain even though vaccination programmes specifically targeting underserved areas of developing countries have been in place for many years.

Inequalities characterizing child and maternal health and mortality are also closely linked to underlying inequalities within the health system, especially differentials in access to prenatal care, skilled care at delivery and emergency obstetric care. Table III.8 shows within- and between-country disparities in women's access to health professionals for the delivery of their babies. In Kazakhstan and Turkmenistan, almost 100 per cent of both urban and rural births are attended by a doctor or other health professional, putting those countries on par with developed countries. In contrast, fewer than 60 per cent of urban births in Haiti, Nepal and Nigeria are attended by a health professional, and the percentage is even lower for rural areas. In some countries large proportions of rural births (19 per cent in Mali and 22 per cent in Rwanda) are attended by no one, raising the risks of both child and maternal mortality.

HIV/AIDS and other diseases

The HIV/AIDS epidemic is worsening in parts of Africa and Asia, while throughout most of Europe and North America significant progress is being made in controlling the epidemic and averting mortality; it is situations such

Table III.10. Women living with HIV: the world and major regions, 2004

Region	*Number of women aged 15-49 years living with HIV*	*Women as a proportion of adults aged 15-49 years living with HIV (percentage)*
World	17.6 million	47
Sub-Saharan Africa	13.3 million	57
Middle East and North Africa	250 000	48
East Asia	250 000	22
South and South-East Asia	2.1 million	30
Latin America	610 000	36
Caribbean	210 000	49
Eastern Europe and and Central Asia	490 000	34
Western and Central Europe	160 000	25
North America	260 000	25

Source: UNAIDS, *AIDS Epidemic Update, December 2004* (http://www.unaids.org/wad2004/report.html; accessed 13 April 2005).

as this that epitomize the strong link between poverty and health inequalities. The number of people living with HIV has been rising in every region, with especially steep increases in East Asia and in Eastern Europe and Central Asia; sub-Saharan Africa, with more than 25 million infected adults and children, has been the region hardest hit by the epidemic (see table III.9) (UNAIDS, 2004). The health and mortality gulf between developed and developing countries will continue to widen, as many of the countries most seriously affected by the HIV/AIDS epidemic have some of the lowest life expectancies recorded in recent history and are likely to experience continued high mortality over the next 50 years, while in the developed world the epidemic will have no perceptible impact on life expectancy.

One important reason for the inequalities generated by the HIV/AIDS epidemic relates to the availability and affordability of treatment. The relatively high cost of antiretroviral therapy prevents poorer individuals and Governments from obtaining treatments that can both reduce the risk of HIV transmission and prolong the lives of those who are already infected. Inequalities in the global pharmaceutical market and in national science and technology infrastructures have contributed to the predicament; poorer countries cannot afford the expensive drug therapies available abroad and are unable to produce cheaper generic equivalents locally, in part owing to their perennial lack of manufacturing capacity.[5]

The impact of the HIV/AIDS epidemic has extended beyond the health sector and, again, has been most widely felt in the poorest countries. The epidemic is linked to widening inequalities in poverty, social status, access to education and employment. In those countries in which HIV/AIDS is most prevalent, the epidemic is rapidly eroding the progress made in reducing within- and between-country gender inequalities in access to educational and employment opportunities. In East Asia, North America, and Western and Central Europe only about a quarter of HIV-infected individuals aged 15-49 years are women, but in sub-Saharan Africa women make up almost 60 per cent of this same group (see table III.10) and around 75 per cent of HIV-infected individuals aged 15-24 years (UNAIDS, 2004).

In addition to being at a disproportionately higher risk of acquiring HIV, females in the regions most seriously affected by the epidemic are more likely to bear the burden of caring for infected or affected family members. Girls, who often assume the responsibility of caring for sick parents and younger siblings, suffer the consequences of a truncated education, early entry into the unskilled labour force, possible exploitation and abuse, and subsequent poverty and social exclusion. The AIDS epidemic threatens to reverse the progress made in the past two decades in reducing the gender gap, particularly in access to education.

Within-country inequalities linked to HIV/AIDS are most evident in the area of human rights. The stigmatization of those infected and affected by HIV/AIDS has led to some of the worst forms of discrimination and isolation within communities. Women are especially vulnerable to discrimination when they become infected with HIV. In addition, inequalities under the law in some areas of the world frequently leave women who survive the death of an infected male relative without access to property or resources, driving them deeper into poverty.

A number of other diseases also contribute to the disparities in health and mortality indicators within and between countries. Malaria, in particular, takes a heavy toll in areas in which the disease is endemic. WHO estimates that malaria kills at least 1 million people every year and contributes to another 2 million deaths. Since about 90 per cent of global malaria deaths occur in sub-Saharan Africa, and the overwhelming majority of those who die are young children, the human and monetary costs of the disease fall heavily on the region.

It is estimated that approximately 2 billion people are infected with the bacteria that cause TB, though healthy individuals may never develop active disease (Global Fund to Fight AIDS, Tuberculosis and Malaria, 2005). Each year there are about 8 million new cases of TB, and approximately 2 million people with suppressed immune systems die of the disease. Although TB is more prevalent in developing countries, it persists in developed countries as well, especially among lower socio-economic groups and those with HIV (United States General Accounting Office, 2000). Lack of compliance with treatment regimens has contributed to the emergence of drug-resistant strains of TB, undermining efforts to bring the disease under control. Drug-resistant strains of TB are present everywhere in the world but are particularly prevalent in Africa, Central Asia and Eastern Europe (United States General Accounting Office, 2000).

In addition to being primary causes of illness and death, both malaria and TB may serve as complicating factors affecting the acquisition, progress or outcome of other diseases. According to the Global Fund to fight AIDS, Tuberculosis and Malaria, one third of people with HIV will also develop TB, as the weakening of the immune system leaves them more vulnerable to opportunistic infections. Most of the deaths associated with TB occur among those between the ages of 15 and 54, depriving communities of their most productive adults.

Hunger and malnutrition

Improvements in agricultural productivity and the development of food manufacturing and preservation technologies during the twentieth century have produced a world of abundance. Since the early 1970s, global food production has tripled and the price of major cereals has fallen by about 76 per cent. There is more than enough food in the world for all its inhabitants, and low-cost food supplies are produced in quantities sufficient to meet the needs of the growing global population. If food was distributed equitably around the world, enough would be available for everyone to consume an average of 2,760 calories a day (*World Ecology Report*, 2005). In spite of these facts and possibilities, appalling nutritional inequalities persist throughout the world.

Food emergencies, which can lead to famines or crises in which starvation from insufficient food intake combined with high rates of disease are associated with sharply increased death rates, have risen dramatically in the past several decades. The number of these emergencies has increased from an average of 15 per year during the 1980s to more than 30 per year since 2000. Most of the crises have taken place in Africa, where the average number of food emergencies every year has almost tripled in two decades. As of July 2004, 35 countries were experiencing food crises requiring emergency assistance (Food and Agriculture Organization of the United Nations, 2004).

In many parts of the world a significant proportion of the population suffers sustained nutritional deprivation, characterized by inadequate intake of protein and micronutrients and by frequent infections or disease. This long-term condition rarely receives media coverage, but more people may die from its indirect effects than from famine. Malnutrition affects around 852 million people worldwide, including 815 million in developing countries, 28 million in transition countries, and 9 million in the industrialized world. In the developing world 20 per cent of the total population is undernourished (Food and Agriculture Organization of the United Nations, 2004).

Malnutrition is one of the primary causes of child mortality, accounting for about half of the 10.4 million child deaths occurring annually in the developing world. Malnourished children who survive often experience the long-lasting effects of disease and disability, reduced cognitive ability and school attendance in childhood, and lower productivity and lifetime earnings in adulthood. The height and weight of almost a third of all children in developing countries fall far enough below the normal ranges for their age to signal chronic undernutrition, and WHO estimates that more than 3.7 million child deaths in 2000 were directly linked to the children being seriously underweight. In economic terms, every year that hunger remains at current levels, developing countries lose around US$ 500 billion or more in productivity and earnings forgone as a result of premature death and disability (Food and Agriculture Organization of the United Nations, 2004). This burden is mainly borne by those who can least afford it, namely the poorest in society.

There are no clear signs that these trends will be reversed anytime soon. According to the Food and Agriculture Organization of the United Nations (FAO), the number of undernourished people in the developing world fell by 27 million between 1990-1992 and 2000-2002 but rose at an annual rate of almost 4 million between 1995-1997 and 2000-2002, seriously offsetting the gains achieved in previous years and resulting in a net reduction of only 9 million for the decade as a whole (1990-1992 to 2000-2002) (Food and Agriculture Organization of the United Nations, 2004).

There are added dimensions to the patterns of inequality characterizing food crises and sustained nutritional deprivation. In these situations, food may not be divided equitably among household members, with women, children (especially girls), and the elderly receiving proportionately less than adult men. Different studies of famines have helped explain the largely human-induced economic, social and political factors that may contribute to food crises. Whether these situations are the result of man-made or natural disasters or a variable combination of the two, they reflect the inability of large groups of people to gain access to food in the societies in which they live, so the impact they have on the population depends on the way society is organized (Dreze and Sen, 1989). A study of the drought-induced famine in Wollo, Ethiopia, describes how the peasantry were engaged in subsistence agriculture and were generally able to manage until rising taxes and other obligations reduced many of them to acute poverty, leaving them with few resources or reserves with which to weather the drought (Dessalegn, 1987).

At the other end of the food spectrum, overnutrition (excessive calorie intake) is also becoming a global problem. There are more than 1 billion overweight adults in the world, at least 300 million of whom are clinically obese (Chopra, Galbraith and Darnton-Hill, 2002). Obesity levels have risen sharply in Australia, Canada, Europe and the United States during the past several decades (Flegal and others, 1998). The issue of overnourishment is addressed further in chapter IV.

Education

Substantial global inequalities persist in the realm of education. Although a number of developing countries, principally in Central Asia, East Asia and the Pacific, Latin America and the Caribbean, and North Africa, are on track to achieving primary school enrolment ratios that are consistent with the Millennium Development Goals, significantly lower levels of educational progress and achievement are still being registered in sub-Saharan Africa and South and West Asia. In many countries school enrolment has improved, though in a number of areas completion rates remain low, especially among girls. Africa, especially sub-Saharan Africa, lags behind other developing regions, and a redoubling of efforts is required to overcome the region's unfavourable initial conditions in terms of human capital.

Table III.11 illustrates the wide disparities in the educational status of household members both within and between selected developing countries.[6] Incorporating two separate groupings, the table shows the countries with the highest and lowest proportions of uneducated males in the household, along with the extent of gender-specific educational inequality within and between countries for urban, rural and all households. Overall, the proportions of male household members who have had no education range from just under 3 per cent in Armenia to more than 70 per cent in Burkina Faso and Niger. Even more striking are the wide disparities in household educational attainment within countries. There are significant urban-rural differentials, with rural residents far more likely to have no education. In virtually every country, female household members in both urban and rural areas are more likely than males to be uneducated.

Existing gaps in the educational attainment of household members reflect decades of unequal educational opportunities. Table III.12 shows the differences in primary school enrolment between world regions. The net primary school enrolment ratio of 84 per cent at the global level conceals the much better performance of Central Asia, East Asia and the Pacific, Latin America and the Caribbean, and North America and Western Europe, all of which have ratios of over 90 per cent for 2001; it also fails to convey the much worse situation in sub-Saharan Africa, where net enrolment is only 62.8 per cent. Female enrolment ratios are generally lower than those of males.

The three regions faring the worst had the most substantial increases in primary school enrolment between 1998 and 2001, and two of them had very large numbers of students enrolled at this level. In sub-Saharan Africa alone, primary enrolment jumped by more than 11 million during this short period. While higher enrolment helps narrow the gaps in access to education, it also places increased pressure on the education systems of countries that are least able to handle it. Consequently, the quality of public education has suffered in many countries, and those who have sufficient resources and opt for a more expensive private education are augmenting their social and economic advantage over the poorer segments of society.

Studies indicate that inequality declines as the average years of schooling increase, with secondary education producing the greatest pay-off, especially for women (Cornia and Court, 2001). Given this fact, the global situation

Table III.11. Percentages of total, urban and rural household populations with no education, by sex

Country	Year	Total			Urban areas			Rural areas		
		Males	*Females*	*Difference (females-males*	*Males*	*Females*	*Difference (females-males)*	*Males*	*Females*	*Difference (females-males)*
Countries with the lowest proportion of uneducated males										
Armenia	2000	2.8	2.9	0.1	2.1	1.9	-0.2	3.7	4.4	0.7
Kazakhstan	1999	4.2	4.9	0.7	3.0	4.0	1.0	5.2	5.7	0.5
Kyrgyzstan	1997	4.2	6.0	1.8	4.1	5.2	1.1	4.3	6.4	2.1
Philippines	1998	4.2	4.3	0.1	2.3	2.3	--	6.0	6.5	0.5
Bolivia	1998	4.9	13.7	8.8	2.0	6.6	4.6	10.3	27.4	17.1
Dominican Republic	1999	4.9	6.4	1.5	3.1	5.0	1.9	7.8	9.2	1.4
Uzbekistan	1996	5.7	6.2	0.5	4.8	5.0	0.2	6.2	7.0	0.8
Paraguay	1990	5.9	7.6	1.7	3.9	5.2	1.3	7.7	10.4	2.7
Turkmenistan	2000	5.9	7.2	1.3	5.3	6.2	0.9	6.3	8.0	1.7
Peru	2000	6.1	12.9	6.8	3.5	7.0	3.5	10.8	24.2	13.4
Countries with the highest proportion of uneducated males										
Côte d'Ivoire	1998/1999	43.6	57.2	13.6	29.7	42.4	12.7	51.7	66.4	14.7
Morocco	1992	43.9	64.9	21.0	25.5	43.4	17.9	60.0	83.1	23.1
Comoros	1996	44.3	59.1	14.8	31.9	45.9	14.0	49.4	64.2	14.8
Eritrea	1995	54.4	67.3	12.9	19.7	36.6	16.9	67.7	80.5	12.8
Chad	1996/1997	56.1	77.7	21.6	39.6	57.9	18.3	62.1	83.4	21.3
Guinea	1999	59.8	76.4	16.6	33.8	51.7	17.9	71.9	87.1	15.2
Ethiopia	2000	61.5	76.7	15.2	24.3	39.8	15.5	67.7	83.9	16.2
Mali	2001	66.0	77.0	11.0	40.4	55.7	15.3	76.0	85.1	9.1
Burkina Faso	1998/1999	72.1	83.9	11.8	32.9	45.3	12.4	79.7	90.8	11.1
Niger	1998	72.7	83.6	10.9	41.9	54.6	12.7	81.0	90.9	9.9

Source: ORC Macro, MEASURE DHS STATcompiler (http://www.measuredhs.com; accessed 23 February 2005).

Table III.12. Inequalities in primary school enrolment: the world and major regions, 1998 and 2001

		Enrolment in primary education				*Net enrolment ratio in primary education (percentage)*					
		Total (thousands)		*Females (percentage)*		*Total*		*Males*		*Females*	
Country or territory	*School-age population 2001 (thousands)*	*1998*	*2001*	*1998*	*2001*	*1998*	*2001*	*1998*	*2001*	*1998*	*2001*
World	648 593	656 538	651 913	47	47	84.2	84.0	87.3	86.5	80.9	81.5
Countries in transition	14 259	15 930	14 767	49	49	84.6	90.1	85.0	90.3	84.1	89.8
Developed countries	67 948	70 406	65 552	49	49	96.4	95.6	96.5	95.4	96.4	95.9
Developing countries	566 386	570 207	569 617	46	46	82.7	82.5	86.3	85.3	78.9	79.5
Arab States	39 396	34 725	36 252	46	46	78.1	81.1	82.3	85.1	73.7	76.9
Central and Eastern Europe	24 079	25 484	23 677	48	48	86.7	88.8	88.1	89.9	85.3	87.7
Central Asia	6 627	6 949	6 667	49	49	87.5	94.1	88.0	95.0	87.0	93.2
East Asia and the Pacific	189 557	219 912	211 108	48	48	96.0	93.7	96.1	93.7	95.8	93.6
Latin America and the Caribbean	58 064	78 585	69 660	49	48	94.2	95.7	94.8	95.6	93.5	95.9
North America and Western Europe	51 664	52 858	49 643	49	49	96.3	95.4	96.3	95.1	96.4	95.7
South and West Asia	170 874	158 096	160 398	44	44	80.2	79.0	87.5	84.7	72.3	73.0
Sub-Saharan Africa	108 332	80 406	91 972	45	46	57.6	62.8	61.4	66.4	53.8	59.2

Source: United Nations Educational, Scientific and Cultural Organization, *Education for All Global Monitoring Report, 2005: The Quality Imperative* (Paris, 2005).

Note: Regional averages are weighted means.

with regard to secondary and higher education is even more disquieting than the situation at the elementary school level. In table III.13, school enrolment statistics for the major regions and the world as a whole are used to show the extent of educational inequality at the secondary level; data on tertiary enrolment are more incomplete and less comparable. The table indicates that net enrolment ratios were significantly lower at the secondary level than at the primary level in 2001. Central Asia, Central and Eastern Europe, and North America and Western Europe had the highest levels of secondary enrolment, with ratios of over 80 per cent, while secondary enrolment in sub-Saharan Africa was a very low 21 per cent. The data for 2001 indicate that females were less likely to be enrolled in secondary school, except in Latin America and the Caribbean and in North America and Western Europe. Between 1998 and 2001 net secondary enrolment among young women improved markedly in Latin America and the Caribbean; Africa also registered a small increase.

Education is typically seen as a means of narrowing inequalities, and among those who receive it, that purpose is served; however, education also represents a medium through which the worst forms of social stratification and segmentation are created. Inequalities in educational attainment often translate into differentials in employment, occupation, income, residence and social class. In Latin America, for example, where inequalities within and between countries are considerable, the wide disparities in occupational earnings are directly attributable to the manner in which the market remunerates those with different levels of education (Instituto de Promoción de la Economía Social, 1999). Although there are differences between countries, those with six years of education earn, on average, 50 per cent more than those with no education, and those with 12 years of education earn more than twice as much as those with no education. The study from which this information is taken notes that educational differentials explain 25 to 33 per cent of the income concentration in the countries of Latin America. Analysis of data from the Netherlands adds an intergenerational perspective by confirming that while a certain degree of mobility exists across income groups from one generation to the next, there is a strong tendency for educational segmentation to persist across generations (de Graaf and Kalmijn, 2001).

In summary, the huge and persistent inequalities in education have far-reaching effects, leading to inequalities in employment, wages, health, power and social integration. To redress educational imbalances and thereby reduce the inequalities they engender or perpetuate, effective policies and programmes that target disadvantaged groups but also focus more broadly on improving educational access and quality for all must be implemented. The gender gap in education requires particular attention to ensure that neither sex is favoured over the other. The quality of education also needs to be addressed.

Table III.13. Inequalities in secondary school enrolment: the world and major regions, 1998 and 2001

Region	School age population (thousands)	Enrolment in secondary education (thousands)				Net enrolment ratio in secondary education (percentage)					
		Total		Female		Total		Male		Female	
	2001	1998	2001	1998	2001	1998	2001	1998	2001	1998	2001
World	752 008	424 925	477 586	46	47	51.3	54.9	..	58.1	..	51.5
Countries in transition	34 524	..	31 272	..	49	..	85.0	..	84.8	..	85.2
Developed countries	84 628	87 210	85 816	49	49	87.9	90.0	87.7	89.5	88.1	90.4
Developing countries	632 856	311 079	358 392	45	46	..	48.5	..	52.4	..	44.4
Arab States	38 975	21 997	24 823	46	46	50.8	55.3	53.5	57.7	48.1	52.9
Central and Eastern Europe	43 829	37 881	38 288	49	48	..	82.7	..	83.4	..	82.0
Central Asia	11 946	5 754	10 406	49	49	81.6	83.6	82.3	84.8	80.9	82.4
East Asia and the Pacific	217 947	137 952	149 732	..	47	..	..	..	..	..	..
Latin America and the Caribbean	66 291	41 871	57 159	51	51	52.9	63.8	50.7	61.9	55.1	65.7
North America and Western Europe	61 486	63 630	63 508	49	50	89.4	89.2	89.5	88.8	89.3	89.6
South and West Asia	221 771	95 750	107 017	41	42	..	..	..	..	..	..
Sub-Saharan Africa	89 764	20 358	24 073	44	44	18.0	21.3	19.7	23.1	16.3	19.4

Source: United Nations Educational, Scientific and Cultural Organization, *Education for All Global Monitoring Report, 2005: The Quality Imperative* (Paris, 2005).

Note: Regional averages are weighted means.

Conclusion

A mixed picture emerges from the recent developments relating to factors that may influence levels of inequality within and between countries. There has been progress, especially in reducing inequalities in health and education, but there have also been significant setbacks. The sources of existing inequalities are often deep-rooted, ranging from economic liberalization policies that have both created and sustained inequalities to sociocultural factors that have impeded efforts to address them.

A number of factors have influenced the patterns and trends examined in this chapter. With respect to income distribution, for example, the evidence clearly suggests that overall gains at the global level derive largely from the exceptional economic growth in China and India; most other countries have not benefited from that growth. Within-country inequality in income distribution has worsened, even for a large group of industrialized countries. Poverty reduction efforts have been reasonably successful in some regions, while the poverty situation has stagnated or deteriorated in others. For example, the number of people in China living on less than US$ 1 a day plummeted from 634 million to 212 million between 1981 and 2000, but in sub-Saharan Africa the ranks of the abject poor increased by almost 90 million over a 10-year period (1990-2000). In Latin America, economic recession and stagnation occurring in the 1980s and 1990s had a significant impact on poverty levels. Among other regions the evidence paints more of a mixed picture.

Many countries continue to face deeply entrenched obstacles and challenges that undermine poverty eradication efforts. At the socio-political level, these inhibiting factors include social exclusion and discrimination, which translate into a lack of opportunities and political power. In some countries poverty is exacerbated by disease and premature mortality, which deprive families and communities of their most productive members. Progress in reducing poverty is constrained in many instances by poor governance and by the burden of geography, particularly for small and landlocked countries. A number of economic factors hinder sustained poverty reduction as well, including low or unevenly distributed economic growth, high unemployment, heavy external debt, trade barriers, high levels of income inequality and commodity dependency.

Economic growth is considered essential for sustained poverty reduction. Liberalization policies, for example, are premised on the expectation that the benefits of increased economic growth will eventually filter down to the poor. There is growing recognition, however, that regardless of how much economic expansion a country experiences, poverty reduction is more likely to take place in countries in which Governments have implemented policies and programmes that promote equality, including initiatives to improve access to resources, income, education and employment.

Non-economic indicators are also linked to the persistence and deepening of various forms of inequality. All of the world's regions have made progress towards achieving education for all; however, large disparities are still evident in access to both primary and higher levels of schooling, and the quality of education remains uneven both within and between countries.

The HIV/AIDS epidemic has exacerbated both economic and non-economic inequalities. Infected and affected individuals and families are becoming increasingly vulnerable; there is often a denial of or failure to enforce legal rights, and many lack access to basic education and health services. The situation is particularly alarming in sub-Saharan Africa; this region, which has been hardest hit by the epidemic, is performing poorly with respect to most economic and non-economic indicators, and the gaps between many countries in the region and the rest of the world are widening.

Gender inequalities are often deeply embedded in the fabric of societies. There are persistent gender gaps in access to education and decent jobs, and in remuneration for equal work. In most countries the numbers and proportions of women in the workforce have risen over the past two decades; however, the narrowing gender gap masks the deterioration in the terms and conditions of work among women (Razavi, 2005). The concentration of women in the lower-paying occupations remains high, which limits both their actual income and their opportunities for advancement (income potential). Women constitute a disproportionate share of the world's poor because they often have limited access to land, capital and labour markets, and they are more likely to be engaged in unpaid housework or low-paid domestic work. Women's unequal access to economic and non-economic opportunities is often at the root of their lower status in many societies, and those who are particularly vulnerable may be subject to abuse and sexual exploitation and rendered voiceless in issues related to their own welfare.

Notes

1 High-income non-OECD countries and territories, as classified by the World Bank, include Andorra, Antigua and Barbuda, Aruba, Bahamas, Bahrain, Barbados, Bermuda, Brunei Darussalam, Cayman Islands, Channel Islands, Cyprus, Faeroe Islands, French Polynesia, Greenland, Guam, Hong Kong Special Administrative Region of China, Isle of Man, Israel, Kuwait, Liechtenstein, Macao, Malta, Monaco, Netherlands Antilles, New Caledonia, Puerto Rico, Qatar, San Marino, Singapore, Slovenia, United Arab Emirates, and Virgin Islands.

2 The World Income Inequality Database (WIID), established and maintained by the United Nations University's World Institute for Development Economics Research (UNU/WIDER), collects and stores information on income inequality for developed, developing and transition countries. The WIID was compiled over the period 1997-1999 by extending the data collected by Klaus Deininger and Lyn Squire for the UNU/WIDER-UNDP project "Rising income inequality and poverty reduction: Are they compatible?", overseen by Giovanni Andrea Cornia, former Director of WIDER. As more observations were added to the database, WIDER decided to make the database available to the public in order to facilitate further analysis and debate on

inequality (see the UNU/WIDER World Income Inequality Database, version 2.0 beta, 3 December 2004).

3 A common measure of national inequality is the Gini coefficient, which assesses the variation across individuals in a particular context. The Gini coefficient ranges from 0 (perfect equality) to 1 (perfect inequality).

4 In analyses conducted by ECLAC and the World Bank it is agreed that regional trends are worsening. However, the analyses differ in defining trends for some of the individual countries. While the World Bank indicates an improvement in the distribution of income in Brazil during the 1990s, ECLAC does not confirm this trend. In addition, the improvement observed by ECLAC in the Gini coefficient for Uruguay is not confirmed by the World Bank. Despite these differences, ECLAC and the World Bank reach the same conclusion for the region as a whole (J.A. Ocampo, "Latin America's growth and equity frustrations during structural reforms", *Journal of Economic Perspectives*, vol. 18, No. 2 [Spring 2004], p. 82).

5 Some of the countries hardest hit by the HIV/AIDS epidemic (including a number of least developed countries) do not have to abide by the provisions of the WTO Agreement on Trade-Related Aspects of Intellectual Property Rights (TRIPS Agreement) until 2016; the Doha Declaration on Public Health states that countries can make use of article 31 of the TRIPS Agreement and produce the drugs they need (the restrictions are on exports of generics). The difficulty therefore lies not in obtaining production rights but in the lack of manufacturing capacity and the limits on the exports of generics from those countries that have to conform with the provisions of the WTO agreements (such as India, which has issued a new law).

6 The table includes data obtained at the household level for developing countries that have undertaken national Demographic and Health Surveys.

Chapter IV

Inequalities and social integration

Inequalities and the lack of opportunities contribute to social disintegration. Many remain excluded from the political process, and the hopes, aspirations and concerns of those who have no chance to express themselves are frequently overlooked and ignored. Entrenched power systems that tend to favour a select minority reinforce these inequalities and discourage social integration.

Ensuring that equal opportunities are guaranteed under the law and in practice is essential for social development, and is especially critical for the empowerment of poor people. Even when the poor and marginalized are invited to express their views, it is unlikely that their needs and interests will be given much policy attention unless mechanisms are in place to ensure the realization of their objectives. Elected institutions should serve as the prime vehicle through which vulnerable groups can secure effective representation.

The most recent wave of globalization has contributed to an increasing homogenization of consumption and production patterns. Globalization has improved the quality of life for many; however, excessive consumption can apply severe pressure on the natural resource base and increase distributional inequalities. The present inequalities and deprivation in both consumption and resource use are likely to be passed on to succeeding generations.

A society characterized by extreme inequalities and the lack of opportunities can become a breeding ground for violence and crime. The widespread and systematic destruction of human life is the ultimate indicator that efforts to improve social integration have failed. This failure manifests itself in a number of different ways, including rampant crime, the high incidence of interpersonal violence and armed conflict. There is seldom one simple reason for the increased tendency towards extreme violence; however, it is clear that inequality, especially horizontal inequality (disparities between groups), increases the likelihood of conflict. Another factor is the inability of a growing number of countries to fully integrate youth into society, especially in terms of employment. Today, almost half of the world population is under 25 years of age, and many developing countries are faced with a younger generation that is much larger than ever before. Most labour markets are unable to absorb all of the young people seeking work; statistically, youth unemployment rates are two to three times higher than those for adults. Faced with such bleak prospects and feeling a sense of injustice, young people often experience anomie and may turn to violent behaviour.

The notion of social integration is not limited by time and space, but represents the understanding that present and future generations are entitled to social justice and equality. The decisions made today affect present and future social integration patterns and the opportunities created therefrom. The notion of intergenerational equity assumes that each generation will look after its own needs in a manner that does not disadvantage or harm the next; future generations should not be neglected or made to pay the price for economic and social policies adopted long before their time. Every generation is a custodian for the next and is also responsible for ensuring the well-being of members of the previous generation once their productive years are past. Each generation is entitled to environmental, cultural, economic and social resources.

Efforts to strengthen security and curtail violence have intensified around the globe, but little has been done to address the socio-economic causes of conflict. Governments have increased defence spending in many countries, often diverting human and financial resources away from development. Thus, there is a risk that security concerns will further marginalize the social agenda at both the national and international levels, especially in times of heightened public concern over real and perceived threats. This situation has compounded the challenges and difficulties analysed in this *Report*, precluding the implementation of comprehensive strategies essential for social development, including the creation of an enabling environment and the strengthening of institutions.

Intergenerational dimensions of inequality

In every society there are certain moral obligations between generations. The notion of an implicit agreement between generations dates back to the Greek philosophers; this intergenerational social contract is based on the presumption that each generation should take care of the other and has constituted a central pillar of many different societies. It has been argued that such a contract among citizens must contain something for everybody (Rawls, 1971). The manner in which the intergenerational contract is currently honoured varies across societies. In most developing countries, intergenerational support is sustained within a wide kinship network and sometimes through community interaction, while in developed countries the State mediates and/or supports the contract to varying degrees.

In most societies there is a general consensus that the State should take the lead in key areas. For example, in many countries, the Government is the primary provider of education and health care. The public sector may also provide social assistance and protection for children, the family, older persons and other vulnerable groups. With the demographic shifts and economic, social and political developments around the world, the nature of intergenerational contracts and relationships is continually evolving. There has been some debate on the issue of intergenerational equity and the "cost" of supporting older persons through State pensions and health-care provision.

As societies and their demographic composition change, there is a need to refocus on the responsibilities of the different generations to each other, and to adjust to the new realities. In developed countries, the present debate on generational issues focuses mainly on the financial obligations of the younger working-age population vis-à-vis preceding and succeeding generations. There is some concern that current systems, if not adjusted, will fail to meet the demands of the many people entering retirement in the coming decades and will place an unsustainable burden on future generations.

The possibility of intergenerational conflict is not entirely unlikely, as the younger members of society may eventually be unwilling or unable to support the older members. This debate is usually framed in economic terms and revolves around the funding of pensions, dissaving, health costs and the reallocation of resources. However, while acknowledging that demographic shifts might require adjustments not only in pension formulas and funding sources but in a broad range of policies, the larger debate from an intergenerational perspective should really be about the nature of the social contract in each country.

There is no consensus on the "affordability" of social protection for older persons. It is argued, in the case of the European Union (EU), that relatively small changes in the benefit structure would keep expenditures at current levels, and that the debates on affordability are really debates about social cohesion, societal concepts and values rather than economic parameters (Cichon, 1997). Some contend that the growing emphasis on promoting self-responsibility, especially for older persons, will undermine intergenerational solidarity and lead to a general weakening of overall social cohesion (Walker, 1993).

Research shows that in developing countries, financing small pensions for older persons benefits not only the recipients but their families as well, as society's elder members consistently invest money in their offspring and younger dependents and contribute to the social capital of future generations (HelpAge International, 2004). Intergenerational coping mechanisms may be adversely affected by the failure to recognize and address the negative impact of certain policies and programmes on the intergenerational support system. It is only recently that Governments in sub-Saharan Africa have begun to acknowledge the fact that huge numbers of grandparents are caring for orphans whose parents died of HIV/AIDS, and in many areas social protection measures are being instituted to allow them to continue to do so, or to improve their capacity to provide better care. Still, many older persons continue to struggle with meagre resources to provide for orphans within the family structure.

The traditional debate surrounding pensions and health-care funding tends to obscure the fact that intergenerational equity is influenced by a multitude of factors. Researchers are now beginning to investigate other intergenerational transfers at both the family/community and macro levels, studying the transmission of poverty and of human, environmental, financial, socio-cultural and socio-political capital, and are also examining the ways in which social and economic structures and norms may positively or negatively affect such transfers (HelpAge International, 2004).

Efforts must be made to balance national budgets over an extended period to ensure the overall equitability of the tax burden across generations, the fair and equal distribution of resources among all age groups, and the provision of essential goods and services for the benefit of all in society. Government debts should be reasonable and manageable; future generations should not be made to pay for present spending habits. Economic, social and environmental policies should complement each other to ensure the well-being of future generations.

Many developing countries are burdened with a sizeable national debt. Much of this debt was accumulated during the 1960s and 1970s, and the decisions taken then continue to affect the policies of today. Debt service as a percentage of GNP remains well over 10 per cent in several countries (United Nations Development Programme, 2004b), seriously constraining current fiscal and social policies and ultimately curtailing the opportunities of future generations.

Some policy makers have been looking at ways to reduce expenditures on State-financed and State-supported programmes essential for intergenerational and social cohesion, while at the same time, demographic trends indicate an increase in longevity in most societies and the coexistence of three and four generations. The combination of reduced social and economic support for older persons and even greater reliance on informal intergenerational coping mechanisms will further undermine the intergenerational contract.

There is a need to move beyond the narrow economic efficiency model in assessing the value and meaning of the intergenerational contract to each society. The value the intergenerational contract brings to society in the form of social cohesion and the readiness of societies to honour their social commitments must be celebrated. Governments need to pursue policy changes that support and sustain an inclusive society and not simply look for ways to cut costs while bemoaning the "burden" older persons represent, thereby ignoring their past and present contributions to society.

Consumption, inequality and social integration

An analysis of consumption patterns can provide insights into individual well-being that complement an exclusively income-based approach to inequality. Such patterns constitute an important measure of exclusion, as they identify who does and who does not have access to resources, goods and services. They also highlight the relative deprivation of certain groups in society, a persistent problem worldwide.

Data reveal that observed rates of growth in household consumption vary widely among regions. Over the past 25 years, household consumption has increased at an average annual rate of 2.3 per cent in industrialized countries and 6.1 per cent in the emerging East Asian economies; in Africa, however, the level of household consumption has decreased by 20 per cent over this period (United Nations Development Programme, 1998).

The wealthiest 20 per cent of the population in the highest-income countries account for 86 per cent of total private consumption expenditures, while the poorest 20 per cent worldwide account for just 1.3 per cent. The inequalities in consumption are illustrated by the fact that the wealthiest 20 per cent have 74 per cent of all telephone lines and consume 45 per cent of all meat and fish, 58 per cent of total energy, and 87 per cent of all paper, while the poorest 20 per cent have only 1.5 per cent of all telephone lines and consume just 5 per cent of all meat and fish, 4 per cent of total energy, and less than 1 per cent of all paper (United Nations Development Programme, 1998).

As these consumption levels imply, the material benefits of global development have largely accrued to the wealthy in the industrialized countries. The consumption gap may narrow somewhat over time, but with the finite natural resources available, it would be impossible for the estimated 2.8 billion people currently living on less than US$ 2 a day to ever match the consumption levels of the richest group.

With the burgeoning of a new elite comprised of those benefiting most from globalization, patterns of consumption have emerged in developing countries that mimic those prevalent in developed countries. Conspicuous consumption is becoming more widespread in many regions of the world as the desire for status and for social distinction at the personal and group levels propels individuals from all segments of society towards greater materialism. Achieving status through consumption is as important to the marginalized as it is to the well-to-do, and the pressures of conspicuous consumption are being increasingly felt as countries become more open to global influences (Sanne, 1997). However, if the consumption practices of the several hundred million affluent people in the world today were duplicated by even half of the projected global population of almost 9 billion in 2050, the impact on land, water, energy and other natural resources would be devastating.

The contrast between what is needed to achieve a decent standard of living in developing countries and what is spent on luxury items is striking. For example, US$ 35 billion is spent annually on perfume and cosmetics in industrialized countries, which is equivalent to half of the total amount of official development assistance (ODA) for 2004 (Organisation for Economic Cooperation and Development, 2003).

Altering consumption patterns is likely to be extremely difficult but is a critical necessity, as the effects of excessive consumption can be socially and environmentally debilitating. It has been stated that "the major cause of the continued degradation of the global environment is the unsustainable pattern of consumption and production, particularly in industrialized countries" (United Nations Conference on Environment and Development, 1992). As developing economies continue to advance, this degradation will accelerate. The consequences of increasing consumption and production are most strongly felt by the poor, as present patterns often have an adverse effect on the development of communities and threaten the health and livelihood of those who depend on immediately available resources to sustain themselves.

Because the poor in developing countries tend to live on marginal lands, they are more vulnerable to the effects of environmental degradation. These areas usually have low agricultural potential and are susceptible to floods, landslides, drought, erosion and other forms of deterioration. Soil salinization has been identified as a major cause of land degradation and is responsible for the global loss of at least three hectares of arable land per minute (Food and Agriculture Organization of the United Nations, 2000).

In Asia and sub-Saharan Africa, 75 per cent of the poor live in rural areas and rely on common lands for their livelihood. In some Indian states the poor acquire 66-84 per cent of what they feed their animals from shared lands. The use of resources such as communal grazing areas and forest lands provides low-income families with between 14 and 23 per cent of their total earnings, while for the wealthier segments of society the corresponding proportion is only 1-3 per cent. A study conducted in Zimbabwe indicates that the poor are dependent on environmental resources for up to one third of their income, and confirms that less financially secure families require more natural resources for their subsistence (Commission on Human Security, 2003). It has been estimated that more than 350 million people are directly dependent on forests for their survival; however, the growing demand for land for agricultural use and for wood and paper production has accelerated the process of deforestation, particularly in developing countries. Once the forests have been harvested, much of the land quickly degrades and is not suitable for long-term farming or grazing (Commission on Human Security, 2003; Roper and Roberts, 1999).

Existing inequalities are compounded by increased environmental vulnerability, and the effects are felt most strongly when natural disasters occur. In the 1990s, more than 700,000 people lost their lives as a result of natural disasters. While this casualty figure is lower than in previous decades, the intensity and frequency of such events and the numbers of those affected have increased substantially. More than 90 per cent of the victims of natural disasters reside in developing countries. In 2002, rains in Kenya displaced more than 150,000 people, and over 800,000 people living in China were affected by the most severe drought seen in a century (United Nations Environment Programme, 2002; Worldwatch Institute, 2003).

The earthquake and tsunami disaster that devastated parts of South-East Asia in late December 2004 demonstrated the effects of unequal socio-economic vulnerabilities. Addressing the General Assembly meeting on the tsunami and the longer-term recovery and reconstruction, the Secretary-General of the United Nations said, "We know from experience that the poor always suffer the most enduring damage from such natural disasters" (Annan, 2005a).

Inequalities in access to resources are also important in relation to man-made disasters. With the increasing land degradation in many regions, millions of people are unable to produce enough food to sustain themselves and their families. Such a situation increases social tensions and vulnerabilities and can trigger both conflict and mass migration. In many developing countries, competition and the struggle for control over scarce resources leads to violent clashes as dominant groups attempt to subdue and marginalize indigenous and tribal peoples that reside in verdant areas in order to secure access to their land and resources (Food and Agriculture Organization of the United Nations, 2005b). Famine can provoke civil war, as demonstrated during the drought in the Horn of Africa in the 1970s, 1980s and 1990s. During prolonged hostilities a vicious cycle is created when conflict further reduces the production of food and access to resources for marginalized groups (Renner, 1999).

The substantial differences in the quality of life between developed and developing countries will persist for many decades, though trends and projections suggest that consumption levels in the latter will slowly rise to match those in the former. It is a realistic presumption that as developing countries move forward, many of the resident poor will aspire to the lifestyles of the more affluent in developed countries. However, to achieve development that is sustainable in the long run, developed countries must demonstrate that resource-efficient, low-pollution lifestyles are both possible and desirable (Schölvinck, 1996).

Some argue that because consumers represent the demand side of the economy, their preferences and choices largely determine the behaviour and output of other economic agents (United Nations, 1996). However, whether consumers have true freedom of choice is open to question. In modern consumer societies, individuals often become locked into consumption patterns and are constrained by the overarching structure of markets and business as well as by intense pressures from commercial marketing on consumption habits (Sanne, 1997). It is becoming increasingly apparent that the demand for goods and services is guided by a multitude of factors and does not always reflect free choice (Jackson and Michaelis, 2003). The dietary changes taking place around the world constitute evidence of the expanding role of the commercial sector in shaping lifestyles. While these changes may not have a direct effect on inequality per se, the indirect impact has socio-economic implications. For example, people are spending more of their disposable income on non-essential foodstuffs, which are often of low nutritional value. In turn, these dietary changes are contributing to an increase in non-communicable diseases, which places an added strain on the health system.

Obesity, in particular, represents a rapidly growing health threat. There are currently more than 1 billion overweight adults worldwide, and 300 million of them are considered clinically obese (World Health Organization, 2005a). In many countries, the combination of urbanization and rising incomes accompanying development has contributed to major changes in nutritional patterns, leading towards "dietary convergence", or the increasing similarity of diets worldwide (Food and Agriculture Organization of the United Nations, 2005a). Trade in foodstuffs has grown enormously; in 2001 it accounted for 11 per cent of total world trade—a proportion higher than that of fuel (Pinstrup-Andersen and Babinard, 2001).

WHO confirms that the shift from traditional foods such as fish and vegetables to "Westernized" diets that are higher in fat, sugar and salt and lower in fibre has contributed to a decline in overall health, noting that developing countries are beginning to witness a marked increase in ailments commonly found in industrialized countries, including heart disease and diabetes. It is estimated that by 2020 these types of illnesses will account for two thirds of the global burden of disease (World Health Organization, 2002).

The younger generation is particularly vulnerable to these unhealthy dietary changes. Obese children are at increased risk of developing hypertension, hypercholesterolemia, atherosclerosis and diabetes, conditions that are predictive of coronary artery disease (Food and Agriculture Organization of the United Nations, 2002). With the increasing incidence of obesity in children, chronic disease will become more prevalent as the population ages (World Health Organization, 2005a). WHO projections indicate that stroke deaths will double in the developing world over the next 20 years. The number of people with obesity-related diabetes is also expected to double, rising to 300 million by 2025, with the developing world accounting for three fourths of these cases (Food and Agriculture Organization of the United Nations, 2002). If projections are accurate, these developments will have an enormous impact on the demand for health-care and support services, placing an added strain on the economy (Brody, 2002).

Violence and inequality

Countries that promote social integration and respect for human rights are less likely to endure armed conflict and more likely to develop and prosper. Development, security and human rights are intrinsically linked and mutually reinforcing. As stated by the Secretary-General of the United Nations, "we will not enjoy development without security, we will not enjoy security without development, and we will not enjoy either without respect for human rights. Unless all these causes are advanced, none will succeed" (United Nations, 2005c).

Although national and international security are necessary conditions for social development, the increased focus on issues such as combating terrorism and organized crime has diverted attention and human and financial resources away from the development process in recent years. There is a risk that the priority given to national security, a highly visible political issue, will further marginalize the development and human rights agendas at both the national and international levels and delay the implementation of comprehensive strategies aimed at building an enabling environment that promotes social development.

One of the most positive aspects of the international climate prevailing in the 1990s was the relative openness of international negotiation (obstructed until the mid-1980s by the strategic security interests dominating the cold war period). The evolution of closer relations and enhanced cooperation within this context allowed the international community to place issues of worldwide concern, such as gender, the environment, HIV/AIDS and social development, at the top of the global agenda. It also engendered a spirit of collective responsibility that culminated in the widespread ratification of the 1997 Mine Ban Treaty, the Optional Protocol to the Convention on the Rights of the Child on the Involvement of Children in Armed Conflict and the Kyoto Protocol to the United Nations Framework Convention on Climate Change. Further, the establishment of the International Criminal Court cemented the shared commitment of Governments to ensure that appropriate steps would be taken to address grave violations of human rights. However, recent events, including acts of terrorism and armed conflicts, have created a new atmosphere of insecurity and religious and ethnic intolerance in many parts of the world that may well undermine the spirit of common responsibility for the protection of human dignity. It is essential that these threats be addressed; however, it must be emphasized that long-term human security cannot be ensured by military means alone.

While the precise nature of the relationship between violence and social integration may not be immediately apparent, and while there are some examples of violence being used as a means of social integration, it is a reasonably safe assertion that violence is most often a symptom of social disintegration. Whether this violence takes the form of individual assaults, armed conflict, or expressions of self-determination, it is an indicator that societies have not successfully fostered the full integration of all their members.

Societies in which violence is used to address grievances, force change or maintain public order and the status quo tend to be those in which social integration is lacking. Societies that generally promote human rights, democratic processes and non-discrimination tend to have less need of heavily armed security or military forces. Societies characterized by respect for diversity, equality of opportunity, solidarity, security and the participation of all people are usually less prone to resort to violence to maintain public order.

Violent crime

There is no simple causal relationship linking poverty and inequality with violence. There are growing indications that increased inequality can have a negative impact on economic growth and contribute to higher rates of violent crime (Bourguignon, 1999; Fajnzylber, Lederman and Loayza, 2002). However, broad generalizations fail to convey the wide variations and more nuanced realities on the ground. Violent conflicts do occur in and between well-off countries, while most poor countries live in peace. Poverty, inequality and deprivation do not necessarily lead to an increase in violent crime or an immediate revolt, but they often remain in people's memories and influence events at later stages. A holistic approach to development, in which security and freedom from violence are intrinsically linked to economic, social, cultural and political justice and equality, represents the context in which violence is analysed in relation to inequality and social integration.

Based on data from over 100 countries, the United Nations Survey of Crime Trends reveals that the number of reported criminal incidents increased steadily between 1980 and 2000, rising from 2,300 to more than 3,000 per 100,000 people (Shaw, van Dijk and Rhomberg, 2003). The increases in overall rates of recorded crime have been most notable in Latin America and the Caribbean, while slower increases have been noted in the Arab States, Eastern Europe and the CIS, and South-East Asia and the Pacific. Data for sub-Saharan Africa are insufficient to identify any clear trends. Crime rates in North America have been declining steadily since the early 1990s (United States Department of Justice, 2004), while the EU has experienced a significant increase in recorded crime since the 1980s, surpassing North America. Recorded crime rates for the EU and North America tend to be twice as high as the global average, indicating a significantly lower propensity to report crime in most other regions (Shaw, van Dijk and Rhomberg, 2003).

In determining levels of activity, homicide is a good proxy for the broader category of violent crime as it is more frequently recorded than other crimes, providing a relatively reliable source for comparison. Generally, countries that are ranked high in terms of human development have homicide levels below the global average, while all those with high levels of homicide (over 10 per 100,000 inhabitants) are either middle-income or developing countries. In Latin America and the Caribbean, homicide levels are very high and relatively consistent (25 per 100,000 inhabitants). Sub-Saharan Africa also shows high levels (17-20 per 100,000 inhabitants), though there is no clear overall trend. Levels of homicide in the EU are comparatively low (under 3 per 100,000 inhabitants), and a similar trend prevails in Canada. The United States experienced a rise in the 1980s and a dramatic decline in the 1990s, with the incidence of homicide dropping from just under 10 per 100,000 inhabitants to 5.6 per 100,000 inhabitants between 1991 and 2001 (United States Department of Justice, 2004). Eastern Europe and the CIS registered the sharpest increases in homicide, with the combined level rising from 5 per

100,000 inhabitants in the mid-1980s to 8 per 100,000 inhabitants in the early 1990s, then declining slightly thereafter. The trend for South-East Asia and the Pacific showed relative consistency, with between 3 and 4 homicides per 100,000 inhabitants. Fluctuations in homicide rates were greater in the Arab States than in other regions, though the rates remained consistently below 4 per 100,000 inhabitants (Shaw, van Dijk and Rhomberg, 2003).

Although data on crime and violence are often scarce and ambiguous, especially in developing countries, there is sufficient evidence to confirm the significant relationship between inequality and crime levels across both countries and time periods (Bourguignon, 1999; Fajnzylber, Lederman and Loayza, 2000). The correlation between crime levels and inequality seems to be particularly high during periods of economic volatility and recession (Fajnzylber, Lederman and Loayza, 2002).

A strong positive correlation between inequality and crime, especially violent crime, is observed across different countries and regions, as well as for specific countries over extended periods. Some believe this can be explained by the theory of relative deprivation, which suggests that inequality breeds social tensions, as those who are less well-off feel dispossessed when comparing themselves with others. The basic premise "is that the necessary precondition for violent civil conflict is relative deprivation, defined as actors' perception of discrepancy between their value expectations and their environment's apparent value capabilities. Value expectations are the goods and conditions of life to which people believe they are justifiably entitled. ... Value capabilities ... are the conditions that determine people's perceived chances of getting or keeping the values they legitimately expect to attain" (Gurr, 1968). Individuals who feel they are disadvantaged and treated unfairly may seek compensation by any means, including crimes against both rich and poor.

Inequality does not always lead to increased violence and is by no means the only explanation for violent crime. However, it does increase the likelihood of violent crime and armed intracountry conflict, especially when it coincides with other factors. For example, the participation of many young people in violent crime and drug trafficking is linked to the intense cultural pressure for monetary success in order to sustain a level of consumption that confers a desired status (Kramer, 2000).

Armed conflict

While it cannot be said that poverty, inequality and the denial of human rights cause or justify assault, terrorism or civil war, it is clear that they greatly increase the risk of instability and violence. Poorer countries are more likely than richer countries to engage in civil war, and countries that experience civil war tend to become and/or remain poor. In a country in which per capita GDP is US$ 250, the predicted probability of war (in a five-year period) is 15 per cent, while the probability is reduced by half for a country with per capita GDP of US$ 600, and by half again (to 4 per cent) for a country with per capita GDP of US$ 1,250 (Humphreys, 2003).

Violence occurs more frequently in hierarchical societies, where there is typically an unequal distribution of scarce resources and power among identifiable groups distinguished by factors such as territory, race, ethnicity and religion. Violence is more common in countries in which levels of inequality are higher. Countries in which poverty and inequality rates are high also tend to have poorer social support and safety nets, unequal access to education, and fewer opportunities for young people.

Although it is agreed that wealth and growth are generally associated with a lower risk of conflict, there is no consensus on whether certain types of growth make conflict more or less likely. Some may contend that inequality is the primary cause of a particular conflict, but there are insufficient data to support or dispute such a claim; typically there are many possible factors that can contribute to violent conflict. When investigating the potential link between levels of inequality and the incidence or absence of conflicts, it should be kept in mind that the most important aspect of inequality in this context may not be inequality between individuals, but rather inequality between groups (horizontal inequality). Armed conflict and civil war are generally more likely to occur in countries with severe and growing inequalities (or perceived inequalities) between ethnic groups.

Certain levels of inequality may create stresses in society but will often be tolerated, particularly when they remain consistent over time. However, rising inequality can increase tensions, and when this is coupled with a lack of institutional capacity to address the widening disparities, violent conflicts become more likely. Ethnic, religious or cultural differences, in themselves, seldom lead to conflict. However, they often provide the basis on which battle lines are drawn, especially when other factors such as social, political or economic inequalities are present. Ethnic identification has proved to be a vital tool for rebel groups seeking to enhance their legitimacy and recruit new members and support.

A society with a balanced distribution of social and economic resources is generally better able to manage tensions with less risk of institutional and social breakdown than is a society characterized by poverty, economic and social disparities, a systematic lack of opportunity and the absence of universal recourse to credible institutions for the resolution of grievances (Organisation for Economic Cooperation and Development, 2001). Change can often lead to social and political dislocations, the erosion of social cohesion and the weakening of traditional authority structures and institutions. Economic and political transitions inevitably raise tensions, especially when the power balance or access to valuable resources shifts among groups.

The number of individuals affected by violence is significant. In 2002 an estimated 1.6 million people died worldwide from intentionally inflicted injuries (World Health Organization, 2004). Men are more likely than women both to cause and to die from such injuries. Globally, suicide accounts for the majority of intentionally caused deaths (873,000), while armed conflicts (559,000) and interpersonal violence (172,000) claim considerably fewer lives (World Health Organization, 2004). This pattern is reflected in all regions except Africa and Latin America, where interpersonal violence and war claim most of those lives lost to intentionally inflicted violence.

In 2004, more than 17 million people were living as refugees or internally displaced persons owing to violence or the threat of violence, down from 21.8 million in 2003. The numbers of people seeking asylum in industrialized countries fell to a 17-year low in 2004 (United Nations High Commissioner for Refugees, 2005b). Among a group of 50 industrialized countries the number of asylum requests fell from 508,100 in 2003 to 396,400 in 2004, a decline of 22 per cent. Since 2001, asylum applications have dropped by 40 per cent (High Commissioner for Refugees, 2005a). Although this would normally inspire optimism, it is likely that the decrease reflects changing methods of dealing with asylum-seekers, such as the fast-track handling and rejection of applications, rather than greatly improved living conditions in the countries of origin. With the tighter security measures and border controls, it has become increasingly difficult for asylum-seekers to reach their final destinations and file their applications, creating the impression that the numbers of asylum-seekers have decreased.

The above notwithstanding, 2004 was considered a reasonably good year in terms of refugees. Most of the 3.2 million people who fled Rwanda in 1994 were able to go back to their homeland, and hundreds of thousands of refugees returned to Angola, Eritrea, Liberia and Sierra Leone during the year. However, even as the global community remembered the 800,000 who died during the Rwandan genocide, more than 70,000 people in the Darfur region of Sudan lost their lives to violence, and at least 1.8 million residents were forced to flee their homes as their neighbours were being raped and slaughtered. Despite the traditional calls of "never again" when commemorating past genocides, the international community proved to be as ill-equipped to deal with intracountry violence in 2004 as it had been 10 years earlier.

There were 19 major armed conflicts in 18 locations in 2003, signalling a slight improvement over 2002, when there were 20 major conflicts in 19 locations, bringing the number of major conflicts down to their second-lowest level since the end of the cold war (Dwan and Gustavsson, 2004). In only two cases were the hostilities between States. Between 1990 and 2003, there were 59 major armed conflicts in 48 locations, only four of which involved war between countries. It should be noted that although many conflicts are classified as internal, they have an international element to them in that warring factions are supported by neighbouring countries. In recent years, most of the conflicts of this nature have taken place in Africa. Of the 25 countries ranked lowest in the human development index in 2004, 23 are in Africa, and 20 are currently or have recently been in conflict.

There is increasing awareness that proactive conflict prevention is more effective and significantly less expensive than conflict resolution for securing national and international peace and preventing the massive loss of life and property. It has been estimated that preventive action in Rwanda in 1994 would have cost about US$ 1.3 billion, while overall assistance to that country in the wake of the genocide cost US$ 4.5 billion (United Nations, 2001). Prevention is both cost-effective and possible; studies have estimated that in the second half of the 1990s there would have been 25 per cent more violent conflicts in the world had preventive measures not been undertaken (Commission for Africa, 2005). The most effective conflict prevention strategies, however, are those aimed at achieving reductions in poverty and inequality, full and decent employment for all, and complete social integration.

Youth demographics

High rates of unemployment and underemployment, especially among youth (aged 15-24 years), contribute to the growth of all types of informal economic activity. The incapacity of a country to integrate younger labour market entrants into the formal economy has a profound impact on the country as a whole, with effects ranging from the rapid growth of the informal economy to increased national instability; in the latter case, organized crime and violent rebel groups are often able to recruit heavily from the huge supply of unemployed youth.

In the year 2000 more than 100 countries were experiencing youth bulges, which occur when young people between the ages of 15 and 24 comprise at least 40 per cent of the national population. All of these youthful countries are in the developing world, with most concentrated in the Middle East and sub-Saharan Africa (United Nations, 2003). Youth bulges, which are associated with high levels of unemployment, poverty and inequality, increase the likelihood of violent conflict within countries (Urdal, 2004). Even under the best conditions, generations that are considerably larger than those preceding them run into institutional bottlenecks. Unemployment tends to be two to three times higher for young people than for the general population, and the lack of work opportunities may cause intense frustration among youth, especially if expectations have been raised through expansions in education. The situation is aggravated when youth bulges coincide with economic downturns, which further limit a country's capacity to absorb additional labour.

This argument is valid for criminal activity in general. Although a higher level of education is normally associated with a lower likelihood of conflict, this can change when unemployment is high. Deep dissatisfaction is especially prevalent in settings in which recruitment processes for political and economic positions are closed, and in which avenues for social change and social justice are open only to the privileged members of certain groups.

Faced with social exclusion, many young people conclude that there is no way for them to influence or change their own situations or society as a whole. Without any real prospects for decent and productive employment, young people may turn to violence. This decision typically has dire consequences for the young people themselves, but also has far-reaching implications for society that should not be underestimated. In February 2005, during an open debate in the Security Council relating to security issues in West Africa, the Secretary-General of the United Nations commented, "Youth unemployment levels are shockingly high, and the accompanying desperation carries a real risk of political and social unrest in countries emerging from crisis, and even in those that are currently stable" (Annan, 2005b).

Most of those who inflict violence on others are males under the age of 30. Young men have committed most of the war crimes and atrocities in history, and it is young men who carry out most of the violence and killing in conflict zones today. Young men tend to make up the rank and file in military and paramilitary forces, and also comprise the majority of civilians involved in violent activity, either alone or in groups. Young people are also particularly vulnerable in times of conflict. They are more likely to be forcefully recruited as combatants and to become victims of human trafficking and targets for sexual violence; in addition, they are deprived of educational and socialization opportunities.

As already indicated, another important element to be incorporated in the analysis is relative deprivation, as opposed to objective deprivation. Poverty alone may not generate grievances or conflict, but individuals and groups may experience strong resentment and be more inclined to engage in violence when they perceive a gap between what they have and what they believe they deserve or what others have. This tendency is particularly pronounced among easily identifiable groups with a strong collective identity based on ethnicity, religion, language or culture.

The attitudes and behaviour of one generation can have a significant effect on the psychological and behavioural development of another. The characteristics, values and outlook of a particular generation can influence the choices made by the next, as well as the outcome of those decisions. The "inheritance" of opportunities has already been addressed, but the intergenerational legacy can also include beliefs and principles, parenting styles, the tendency towards fidelity or adultery, and even depression, trauma and violence. This phenomenon often exacts a social price. Perceptions are frequently passed down through the generations, which may result in a deepening of discrimination against particular ethnic or religious groups or against persons with disabilities, for example. For those who inherit mental illnesses or negative behavioural tendencies, there are actual costs associated with rehabilitation and social costs associated with leaving them untreated. A particularly high price is paid by those who receive such a legacy; if individuals are exposed to negative or damaging influences at an impressionable age, the effects and implications can extend throughout their lifetime and that of their descendants.

Rape and child soldiers

Rape has accompanied war and other forms of conflict throughout history. Sometimes it occurs with the breakdown in law and order as armed combatants in a position of relative power take advantage of unarmed civilian women. At times, however, sexual assault is a part of a group's or Government's policies. It has been a consistent feature of religious crusades, revolutions, liberations, wars of imperial conquest and genocides. It is used to punish enemies and reward victors. In war, as in peace, it is the most vulnerable members of society, including women, refugees, minority groups, the young and the poor, who suffer disproportionately from sexual assault.

On the subject of protecting women and girls from rape and sexual violence in conflict situations, the most that can be said is that the international community is now more aware of the need for such protection. "The problem is as serious as it has ever been" (United Nations Children's Fund, 2005). Since the high-profile accounts of systematic rape by soldiers in the Balkans in the 1990s, there has been a growing general awareness of the prevalence of rape as an instrument of war in general and of genocide in particular. Nevertheless, the practice continues and has been an element of virtually every single recent conflict.

Although there are widely diverse social and cultural attitudes towards rape and particularly towards the victims of rape, the effects on the victims' societies are remarkably similar. The physical and psychological damage to those who have been violated is catastrophic and can never truly be measured. During times of conflict the perpetrators of rape and other forms of sexual assault are aware of the harm done not only to the victim but to the enemy community as a whole. Rape is frequently used as a deliberate strategy to destroy family and community bonds and therefore constitutes a tool of "ethnic cleansing" or genocide. It is deliberately used to infect women with HIV/AIDS and other diseases, which often exposes the victims and their families, including their children, to social exclusion and stigmatization, ensuring that they and their communities continue to suffer from the crimes years after they are perpetrated. Children born as a result of rape often endure stigmatization, discrimination and exclusion from their communities. These circumstances reflect an intergenerational dimension of social disintegration whereby the consequences of crimes committed against one generation are also suffered by the victims' descendants.

A number of underlying factors make sexual violence in conflict extremely difficult to eradicate. The subordinate status of women in peacetime often deepens in times of conflict, making them even more vulnerable to sexual abuse. Little progress has been made in bringing the perpetrators to justice, and because there are inadequate services for the survivors of sexual assault, their reintegration into society often proves enormously difficult (Human Rights Watch, 2004).

Child soldiers represent another direct result of a society's failure to ensure social integration. Just as rape is used as a deliberate weapon or strategy in conflict, the use of child soldiers is based on a deliberate policy of exploitation; essentially, children are seen as cheap, compliant and effective fighters. Human Rights Watch estimates that there are around 300,000 child soldiers in at least 20 countries, and despite increasing awareness and improved understanding of policies that can address the use of children in war, that number has remained fairly constant in recent years (Human Rights Watch, 2004). The recruitment (more accurately described as the abduction) of children for the war in the Democratic Republic of the Congo increased dramatically in late 2002 and early 2003, while the end of the wars in Angola and Sierra Leone freed thousands of children from active armed conflict.

Increased awareness of the situation of child soldiers has led to the adoption of three important treaties in recent years.[1] These international treaties have been almost universally embraced but have proved difficult to enforce. Non-State armed groups constitute a particular challenge, as little can be done to induce compliance. These groups are less sensitive to world opinion, and since there is no real threat of military aid being cut off or sanctions being imposed against either these types of groups or formal Governments for their use of child soldiers, there is no reason to expect any significant improvement in the near future.

Halting the use of child soldiers must go hand in hand with the full reintegration of these children into society. Former child soldiers are likely to have been denied a formal education and the opportunity to acquire income-generating skills. Often, their participation in conflicts has provided them not only with a way to earn an income but also a sense of community or camaraderie and status. These young people need a viable alternative to participation in armed conflict—one that meets all their basic needs. Up to now, such reintegration components have received less financial support than disarmament and demobilization efforts, creating an imbalance that may lead to increased frustration and further violence (United Nations Children's Fund, 2005).

Domestic violence and slavery

Another insidious symptom of the lack of social integration is domestic violence. Although men are sometimes subjected to domestic violence, women constitute the overwhelming majority of victims. Domestic violence is a serious problem worldwide; research indicates that as many as 69 per cent of women around the globe have been victims of physical assault by a male partner. Physical violence, frequently accompanied by psychological and sexual abuse, has a profound impact on individuals and even entire communities (World Health Organization, 2002).

Although domestic violence occurs in all socio-economic groups, women living in poverty appear to be disproportionately affected; further study is needed to determine why this is the case. Research suggests that domestic violence is caused and sustained by the political, social, economic and structural inequalities between men and women in society, and by the rigid gender roles and power relations between the sexes (United Nations Development Fund for Women, 2003).

Violence between partners in a marital or consensual union is often not perceived to be as serious a crime as violence between two strangers. This perception is prevalent among both public officials and the general population (Iadicola and Shupe, 2003). Largely through the efforts of civil society, legal mechanisms and various public and private programmes have been introduced in many countries to combat domestic and other forms of violence against women (Jelin and Díaz-Muñoz, 2003). Legal and policy reforms usually constitute the first step, though little headway will be made unless these measures are enforced and are accompanied by changes in institutional culture and practice. Ultimately, however, violence against women will not be eradicated until structural inequalities between men and women and general attitudes in society are addressed (Chopra, Galbraith and Darnton-Hill, 2002).

Another challenge facing global society is modern-day slavery. Human trafficking and slavery are among the most extreme examples of the damage inflicted by inequality.[2] The times of individuals claiming legal ownership of other human beings are all but gone, yet slavery still exists and is actually growing at an alarming rate. The magnitude of trafficking and slavery is extremely difficult to measure, given the illicit and clandestine nature of these practices. It is estimated that between 12 million and 27 million people are trapped in forced labour or slavery today (Bales, 2000; International Labour Conference, 2005). Most of these individuals live in debt bondage, serving as human collateral against loans that, in practice, are all but impossible for them to repay; often such debts are inherited by the labourers' children.

It is estimated that 600,000 to 800,000 people are trafficked across borders each year. International trade in human beings as a commodity is believed to generate up to US$ 10 billion per year, an amount exceeded only by the proceeds of the illegal trade in drugs and arms (United States Department of State, 2004; United Nations Children's Fund, 2005). These figures do not take into account individuals who are trafficked within national borders, as they are even more difficult to identify. The United Nations Population Fund (UNFPA) estimates that the total number of people trafficked within and across borders may be as high as 4 million (United Nations Population Fund, 2005). Eighty per cent of trafficking victims are women and girls, and a large majority end up being exploited in the commercial sex industry. UNICEF has estimated that 1.2 million children are trafficked each year, usually for sexual exploitation or domestic labour (United Nations Children's Fund, 2004).

The link between poverty/inequality and slavery is remarkably simple. Individuals from families living in poverty are sold as goods to satisfy the demand for cheap labour. Poverty and the vulnerability it creates are key in this context. Traffickers use force, fraud or coercion to trap and then exploit their victims, who are usually women and children. The victims are confined by means of violence and the threat of violence, fear of the authorities (especially if they have been illegally transported to another country), drug addiction, shame and family obligations. Once a slave ceases to be profitable, he or she is discarded and easily replaced with another human being living in poverty. Trafficking in women and girls ranks among the three top sources of income for organized crime (Heyzer, 2002; United Nations Development Programme, 1999). The fact that trafficking has become such a lucrative business with relatively low risks, combined with the difficulties in identifying victims and traffickers, clearly presents a problem in combating this crime.

Notwithstanding the considerable challenges, various actions can be and have been taken to prevent trafficking, including strengthening cooperation between transit and destination countries, targeting the demand side of sexual slavery, and reforming immigration laws to protect victims of trafficking and allay their fears of deportation. Governments are increasingly identifying trafficking as a crime, and public awareness of the problem is growing. Nonetheless, any progress made in this area is likely to be hard-won. There remains a huge demand for immigrant and trafficked labour, and there is an equally large supply of cheap and disposable human beings that may be easily procured by means of deception, coercion and force to meet this demand. The demand comes from the more prosperous segments of society, and the supply is met by the people living in poverty; the driving force in this equation is the relative inequality between communities, countries and regions.

Fostering democracy and social integration

Promoting respect for democracy, the rule of law, diversity and solidarity can contribute to the elimination of institutionalized inequalities and is therefore critical to successful social integration. Countries that provide opportunities for all people to voice their grievances peacefully and allow them to participate in the political process and influence policy formulation, implementation and monitoring are less likely to experience internal conflict. Some contend that the true meaning of democracy is the ability of a person to stand in the middle of a town square and express his or her opinions without fear of punishment or reprisal. This takes democracy beyond the institutional definition to include tolerance and acceptance at the individual and group level. It also underscores that democracy cannot be imposed by an outside source. Where democratic institutions are not permitted to flourish, and where there are no outlets for peaceful dissent, specific groups become marginalized, social disintegration is rife, and there is a greater chance for political upheaval.

Democratic, transparent and accountable governance is indispensable in achieving social development. There are now more democratic countries and a greater degree of political participation than ever before. The 1980s and 1990s witnessed what has been called the "third wave" of democratization. In 1980, 54 countries with a total of 46 per cent of the global population had some or all of the elements of representative democracy. By 2000, these figures had risen to 68 per cent of the world's population in 121 countries. However, there is some scepticism about the consolidation of newly planted roots of democracy in some regions; the momentum gained during the 1990s appears to be slowing and in some places may be receding (United Nations Development Programme, 2002).

Democratic political participation consists of more than voting in elections. The ideal of "one person, one vote" is often undermined by unequal access to resources and political power. Thus, there is a danger of decreased motivation to participate, demonstrated by low voter turnouts, unequal capacities to participate in the democratic process and ultimately unequal capacities to influence policy outcomes. Formal political equality does not necessarily create increased capacities to participate in political processes or influence their outcomes, and the transition to democracy does not in itself guarantee the protection or promotion of human rights.

Civil, cultural, social, economic and political rights are essential for maintaining a democratic society. These human rights are mutually reinforcing and must include freedom of association, assembly, expression and participation for all citizens, including women, minorities, indigenous peoples and other disadvantaged groups.[3] Respecting and upholding human rights is crucial not only for the well-being of individuals, but also for the active engagement of citizens and the well-being of society. If democracy is to flourish, it is not enough to enshrine these freedoms in legislation; they must be backed up and protected by policies and political will to ensure that all people have the opportunity to participate actively in the processes that affect their everyday lives.

Democracy is not an achievement but a process that must be continually reinforced at all stages by the internal actions and institutions of the State as well as by the international community. It is necessary to operate under the assumption that democracy is within the reach of any country or region. It is also essential to acknowledge that democratization does not mean the homogenization of cultures; in a true democracy diversity is a source of enrichment and empowerment. One of the fundamental principles of democracy is the right of all individuals to freely express and defend alternative viewpoints both privately and in the context of political participation. In light of the tremendous benefits at all levels, opportunities to strengthen democratic institutions should not be missed.

Participation is central to the development process and is essential for its success and sustainability. Although often overlooked in the past, marginalization has emerged as a critical element in the re-evaluation of poverty reduction strategies. Nonetheless, many policy prescriptions are still designed without adequate analysis of how they might affect the poor. The most vulnerable groups in society, including the poor, remain outside the sphere of political activity and influence, excluded from the formulation, implementation and monitoring of the very policies developed to address their plight. As a result, poverty reduction programmes may suffer from an urban bias, despite the fact that three quarters of the world's poor live in rural areas (International Fund for Agricultural Development, 2004).

In some countries, stakeholders have successfully advocated for an increase in the share of public resources allocated to social development. However, even in countries in which poverty programmes have been developed through widespread consultations, the priorities identified are not necessarily linked to budget mechanisms, and the final programmes may fail to target the poorest.

Enhancing women's political participation is one means of achieving social empowerment. In 2003, women held only 15 per cent of national parliamentary seats worldwide, an increase of slightly less than 2 percentage points since 1990. The Nordic countries have come closest to achieving gender parity in political representation; in 2003, women comprised 40 per cent of national parliamentarians, more than double the average for developed countries as a group (United Nations, 2004c). Excluding half the population from the political process represents a poor use of human capital and is ultimately a recipe for poorer performance at all levels. Socio-economic obstacles to women's political participation include poverty or inadequate financial resources, limited access to education, illiteracy, limited employment options (in terms of both work opportunities and choices of profession), unemployment, and the dual burden of domestic duties and professional obligations.

The proportion of a country's budget earmarked for the needs of women and girls is often an accurate indicator of the country's priorities. Budgets are never gender-neutral, and in recent years it has been recognized that gender-responsive budget initiatives represent a tool for promoting gender equality and the human rights of women in numerous countries (United Nations Development Fund for Women, 2001).

Indigenous peoples have been discriminated against throughout history and are still frequently denied their basic human rights, in particular their cultural rights and the right to exercise control over their land and natural resources. They are often excluded from the political process. It is critical to ensure their participation so that their concerns can be addressed and another step can be taken towards the achievement of a more equitable society.

Persons with disabilities have also been consistently discriminated against and left without an opportunity to engage actively in the political process. Studies indicate that individuals with disabilities are up to 10 times more likely than others to become victims of crimes, often perpetrated by family members or care providers (Petersilia, 2001). The current consultations for the Comprehensive and Integral International Convention on the Protection and Promotion of the Rights and Dignity of Persons with Disabilities represent an important step in ensuring the protection of this group's fundamental human rights.

Policy discussions on youth and older persons often reflect an underestimation of their contributions to society and a lack of understanding of their needs. To ensure an inclusive democracy that promotes intergenerational equality, these groups must be integrated into the entire policy-making process.

Conclusion

In many places, social integration remains a distant ideal. Communities worldwide have had to endure enormous pressures as a result of the social changes brought about by globalization. Increases in poverty and inequality and the decline in opportunities have had a serious adverse effect on the well-being of individuals, communities and even countries. It is widely felt that socio-economic needs are not being addressed; few believe that State institutions act in their best interests, and many communities are dissatisfied with their economic situation. Negative perceptions of community well-being and future prospects can leave many discouraged, making it difficult to ensure the participation and investment of all members of a society in the development process.

Since the events of 11 September 2001, global security has risen to the top of the international agenda and has become a focus of increasing concern among the general population. In an international survey conducted by the World Economic Forum, 45 per cent of the respondents felt that the next generation would live in a less safe world, while only 25 per cent believed that the world would be a safer place for future generations (World Economic Forum, 2004). The Middle East and Western Europe were the most pessimistic about future security; Africa, Eastern and Central Europe, and Western Asia were the only three regions that displayed higher levels of optimism than pessimism.

Accompanying this growing perception of increased insecurity is an expansion in the privatization of security. As previously noted, globalization, deregulation and the weakening of the State are contributing to the growth of the informal economy, and these trends are affecting the criminal black market and the growth of the private security sector.[4] Three interlinked trends in the growing privatization of security and violence have been identified; they include the increasing availability of small arms to the public, the expansion of private security arrangements and the increased involvement of mercenaries in armed conflict (Klare, 1995). While most large-scale weaponry remains under State control, the same cannot be said of the many different types of small arms used in the low-intensity conflicts that have taken place since the end of the cold war. Three in five of the estimated 640 million firearms in the world are held by civilians (Commission on Human Security, 2003).

Surveys conducted in Africa, East Asia, Europe and Latin America indicate that a growing majority of individuals feel they have no control or influence over the economic, political and social factors that affect their lives. Economic and security concerns are causing a great deal of anxiety, and there is little confidence in the ability or commitment of State institutions to manage these growing problems. Countries that have recently undergone profound changes tend to display higher levels of optimism (World Economic Forum, 2004).

Negative perceptions of political processes indicate that increased efforts are required to integrate all segments of society in political life. It is imperative that all individuals have equal access and opportunities to participate in the political process, not only for the sake of justice, but also to ensure that full advantage is taken of a country's human resources and to promote peace and stability. Empowering local groups to take part in the building and improvement of their own communities will make development projects more effective. Involving people in the decision-making processes that affect their daily lives and well-being will significantly reduce the risk of conflict.

The process of social integration is likely to become even more difficult with the demographic and economic changes expected to occur over time. The intergenerational contract, which has provided an effective system of mutual support over the centuries, will be seriously challenged in the coming decades. Many believe that the demographic shifts occurring around the world have ominous implications; the perceived societal threat is often framed in apocalyptic terms that portend power struggles. While changing social, economic and political realities represent an enormous challenge for every society, appropriate planning and sound policy implementation can create opportunities to ensure the well-being of all.

Social integration is a social issue, but it is also an economic, environmental, political, security and human rights issue. The creation of peaceful and productive societies requires the achievement of social integration based on respect for human rights, the principle of non-discrimination, equality of opportunity and the participation of all people, with account taken of the rights and needs of both present and future generations.

Notes

1 The Rome Statute of the International Criminal Court defines the conscription, enlistment or use in hostilities of children under the age of 15 as a war crime; the Worst

Forms of Child Labour Convention, 1999, prohibits the forced recruitment of children under 18 years of age for use in armed conflict; and the Optional Protocol to the Convention on the Rights of the Child on the involvement of children in armed conflict establishes 18 as the minimum age for participation in armed conflict.

2 For a definition of trafficking, see article 3 of the Protocol to Prevent, Suppress and Punish Trafficking in Persons, Especially Women and Children (also referred to as the Palermo Protocol), supplementing the United Nations Convention against Transnational Organized Crime.

3 The issues of these social groups are extensively addressed in the Report on the World Social Situation, 2003.

4 It is questionable whether differentiation between the black market and the informal market is necessary or useful, given that neither is regulated and both are generally outside the reach of the law and are illegal to one degree or another. These essential similarities aside, there is certainly a difference between the market trader selling agricultural products who fails to pay the State sales tax and the small arms trader who provides rebel groups with automatic weapons.

Chapter V
The changing context of development and inequality

Previous chapters build the case for focusing on inequality, highlighting the stark contrasts within and between countries. It is appropriate at this juncture to explore the dynamics underlying this unwelcome reality.

National and international events and circumstances have had a major impact on the pace and level of social development. Globalization stands out as one of the most important phenomena influencing social development in the twenty-first century; of particular significance is the asymmetry of globalization, which has led to the emergence of "winners" and "losers". The new international trade regime has serious implications for the hopes raised at the World Summit for Social Development in 1995. Structural adjustment programmes and market reforms have shaped the economic and institutional context in which financial and trade liberalization have unfolded in recent decades. These changes have generally had a negative impact on the welfare of individuals, groups and communities worldwide, and have some negative implications for future development.

With the combined challenges of globalization and market reforms, including financial and trade liberalization, it becomes evident that the path towards social development can only be charted once the political and institutional dimensions of the current international context are better defined and any shortcomings identified and addressed. Clearly, the quality of governance and of policies formulated within national frameworks can either promote or impede social development. One pressing issue requiring closer attention is financing for development.

Theories of economic convergence suggest that the increasing integration among countries brought about by globalization will promote the convergence of income levels and a consequent reduction in overall income inequality (Barro, 1991; Barro and Sala-i-Martin, 1992; Ben-David, 1993). Existing evidence seems to refute this premise, however, and some studies question whether globalization in its current form can contribute to reducing inequalities worldwide.

Globalization: asymmetries and the loss of policy space

The current global economic system is circumscribed by an international agenda dominated by the issues of free trade, intellectual property rights, financial and capital account liberalization, and investment protection. Conspicuously absent from the agenda are items of critical importance to developing countries, including international labour mobility, international taxation of capital income, financing mechanisms to compensate marginalized countries and social groups, and mechanisms for ensuring macroeconomic policy coherence among industrialized countries and a consequent reduction in the exchange rate volatility among major currencies. The same issues tend to be assigned varying levels of priority and urgency by different groups of countries, and market competitiveness can place countries in direct opposition to one another. For example, products of vital economic importance to developing countries, such as agricultural and labour-intensive manufactured goods, are given the highest levels of trade protection in developed countries, as evidenced by the provision of massive subsidies. In addition, service negotiations remain focused on products and services of major concern to developed countries, including telecommunications and financial services, while modalities that are of particular interest to developing countries, such as the mobility of labour (particularly unskilled labour) for the provision of services, are neglected (Ocampo and Martin, 2003).

One of the more important asymmetries relates to the unbalanced agenda underlying the current process of globalization; more precisely, there is a contrast between the rapid pace of economic globalization and the relative weakness of the international social agenda (deriving largely from the very poor accountability and enforcement mechanisms in the realm of social development). There is increasing recognition of the need to provide the necessary space in the international system for the protection of political, social, economic and environmental "global public goods" (Ocampo, 2005).

As implied in this *Report*, the "policy space" in most countries is somewhat constricted under the current international trade and financial system. Global competitive pressures tend to restrict a country's policy choices and often have an adverse effect on social development, since decisions or actions required to advance social policies and social equality are usually perceived as unnecessary costs. Put simply, social development policies are often mistakenly considered to be in conflict with the preservation of a country's international competitiveness.

The desire of developing countries to attract foreign investment and expand exports has frequently led to a "race to the bottom" in which labour protection and environmental standards are ignored or compromised to make the countries more competitive in the international market. As this suggests, external competitive pressures have restricted the ability of some countries to pursue certain aspects of social policy and have therefore undermined the progress of social development.[1]

Noting the prevailing asymmetries in the world economy, the United Nations Conference on Trade and Development (UNCTAD), in the Plan of Action adopted at its tenth session in Bangkok in February 2000, calls for enhanced bilateral and multilateral efforts to safeguard vulnerable populations and for the benefits of globalization to be more widely shared, stating that "there is no automatic process by which the income levels of developing countries will converge towards those of developed countries" (United Nations Conference on Trade and Development, 2000, para. 4). The Plan of Action stresses the importance of effective social policies for economic growth, noting, for example, that "good health and the attainment of basic education are essential building blocks of development and indispensable for reducing poverty and inequality" (United Nations Conference on Trade and Development, 2000, para. 9).

At its eleventh session, held in São Paulo in June 2004, UNCTAD "built on its previous session by appealing for more coherence between national development strategies and global economic processes in order to achieve economic growth and development. It emphasized that most developing countries have not benefited from globalization and are still facing major challenges in realizing their economic potential, developing their productive sectors and creating employment for a large proportion of their population" (United Nations Conference on Trade and Development, 2004b).

In addition, "the debate focused on ways to make trade work for development, particularly the capacity of international trade to contribute to poverty alleviation and reduce instability in world commodity prices" (United Nations Conference on Trade and Development, 2004b). These themes were reiterated by the ILO in the 2004 report of the World Commission on the Social Dimension of Globalization, "which stressed the importance of policy coherence in achieving a far more inclusive globalization" (International Labour Organization, 2004).

While UNCTAD emphasized at its eleventh session that "development was the primary responsibility of each country, it also recognized that domestic efforts should be facilitated by an enabling international environment based on multilaterally agreed and applied rules" (United Nations Conference on Trade and Development, 2004b). The Conference concluded that "to achieve ... sound global economic governance ... it was necessary to improve coherence between national and international efforts and between the international monetary, financial and trade systems, so that they were more capable of responding to the needs of development" (United Nations Conference on Trade and Development, 2004b).

Some aspects of the current international agenda pose special challenges for developing countries. A prime example is the World Trade Organization (WTO) Agreement on Trade-Related Aspects of Intellectual Property Rights (TRIPS Agreement). Although the basic presumption is that effective protection of intellectual property rights will increase technical innovation and the transfer of technology, there are recent indications that the Agreement may actually restrict technology transfer and jeopardize the interests of poorer countries to protect those of richer countries. More broadly, the TRIPS Agreement may increase the cost of, and thus narrow the range of modalities for, transferring technology to developing countries.

Liberalization policies implemented in many countries in the past couple of decades have produced important changes in the labour market and in labour laws and institutions, including a shift towards greater wage flexibility, the downsizing of public sector employment and a decline in employment security and protection. These changes have led to expanded informal employment, higher labour mobility and less job stability. There has also been greater diversification of the issues of particular concern to workers, and a decline in the importance and bargaining power of trade unions and other labour institutions.

The changes highlighted above have contributed significantly to increases in wage inequality and overall within-country inequality, especially in medium-income developing and transition economies and OECD countries (Cornia and Court, 2001). In view of the fact that wages constitute around 60-70 per cent of total income in most developed countries, this rising earnings inequality is an important component of the increase in overall income inequality.

In many cases, there has been a drop in real minimum wages and a sharp increase in the highest incomes. Among industrialized economies, the widening of the income gap has been especially marked in Canada, the United States and the United Kingdom, where the share of the top 1 per cent of income earners has risen sharply (Atkinson, 2003). In the United States, this group's share reached 17 per cent of gross income in 2000, a level last seen in the 1920s (International Labour Organization, 2004). In developing and transition economies, the rise in earnings inequality has followed a similar pattern. In Brazil and Mexico, for example, trade liberalization has caused wages to decline, especially among unskilled labour, further increasing the wage gap between skilled and unskilled workers (International Labour Organization, 2004). The liberalization of trade has widened the wage gap in six of the seven Latin American countries for which reliable wage data are available, as well as in the Philippines and Eastern Europe (Lindert and Williamson, 2001). Data indicate that in the OECD, Latin American and transition economies, the rise in wage inequality was particularly dramatic between the mid-1980s and mid-1990s, though the extent of the problem varied (Cornia, 2004).

The impact of liberalization and stabilization policies on inequality

Foremost among the global dynamics that help explain the root causes of persistent inequality trends are the liberalization policies implemented in many countries during the past two decades. These reforms have been applied by countries worldwide and have had a major adverse impact on inequality trends.

Many of the new policies and measures adopted to enhance economic performance have not contributed to a more balanced distribution of the benefits of economic growth, but have in fact exacerbated inequalities. Available data indicate that the OECD countries that have applied the strictest regimes in implementing these policies have been among those that have exhibited the greatest increase in within-country inequality in recent decades (Weeks, 2004).

The liberalization and adjustment policies implemented over the past two decades have contributed to the rise in inequality in several ways. The subsections below outline some of the components of these policies and provide insight into the negative impact they have had on income distribution within the countries concerned and worldwide. The review concentrates on two of the more salient elements of these policies: financial liberalization and trade liberalization.

The current international economic approach evolved in the 1980s as the market-guided development perspective gained dominance. As noted in previous chapters, this approach to development was based on the premise that market forces would lead to the most efficient allocation of resources, resulting in faster economic growth and ultimately an improvement in overall development.

The financial crises of the 1990s and the subsequent economic recessions in Asia, Latin America and the Russian Federation demonstrated the social devastation that could result from unrestricted, and at times heavily speculative, international capital flows coupled with procyclical macroeconomic policies. The human impact of these crises—including increased unemployment, poverty and inequality, and the erosion of social cohesion in many countries—underscores the crucial importance of fostering social development.

Experience with structural adjustment programmes exposed the drawbacks of pursuing economic liberalization policies at the expense of social policies. Analysis of the impact of IMF/World Bank structural adjustment and macroeconomic stabilization reforms found increases in poverty during periods of recession (Easterly, 2001). As mentioned in the first chapter, policy makers gradually realized the need for a change, which culminated in the introduction of the World Bank Poverty Reduction Strategy Papers (PRSPs) and the IMF Poverty Reduction and Growth Facility (PRGF).

Further to the development and adoption of poverty reduction strategies with pro-poor and pro-growth programme measures supported by more equitable government budget allocations and increased fiscal flexibility, a new feature of the PRGF is the use of social impact analysis in connection with major macroeconomic and structural reforms. Internal reviews indicate, though, that the systematic incorporation of such analysis into programme design remains one of the areas most in need of improvement (see, for example, World Bank, 2004c; International Monetary Fund and International Development Association, 2003).

External reviews of the PRSP and PRGF initiatives point to heightened concern among civil society organizations over the imposition of structural adjustment conditionalities, given their proven negative impact on poverty. There is also criticism that the IMF and World Bank have not backed up their stated commitment to poverty and social impact analysis with actual implementation. For example, a review by the Nordic Governments of the PRSP process revealed only a nominal linking of macroeconomic and structural adjustment measures with poverty reduction and also a failure to rely on empirical evidence in the adoption of actual policies (Norwegian Agency for Development Cooperation, 2003). These findings led the World Bank to acknowledge an "implementation gap" between planning and action, or more precisely, the disconnection between the discourse on incorporating social dimensions (particularly poverty reduction) in economic programmes and actual practice (World Bank, 2004c).

Financial liberalization

Since the mid-1980s, most developing countries have taken steps to liberalize their domestic banking and financial sectors and open their markets to international capital flows. These processes have been an important cause of the increased poverty rates and inequalities in income distribution documented by various studies. Analysis by the World Bank shows that financial crises have a negative impact on wage distribution, and that this effect persists even after economic recovery (World Bank, 2000). Another study suggests that in Latin America the implementation of financial liberalization measures had the strongest disequalizing impact on wage differentials (Behrman, Birdsall and Szekely, 2000).

Financial liberalization has increased the level of instability and the frequency of financial crises, especially in developing countries (Caprio and Klingebiel, 1996). For example, the liberalization of international capital flows has made countries more vulnerable to capital flight. The flow of capital into a country following the liberalization of its financial system tends to lead to real exchange rate appreciation, which is often linked to higher real interest rates. Higher interest rates often attract additional capital flows. The resulting credit expansion can trigger a consumption and import boom or a speculative asset price bubble. "The demand expansion may prove to be short-lived, if the consequent widening of the external balance is unsustainable, or if capital flees the economy when the bubble begins to deflate" (Taylor, 2004). In short, countries that have undertaken capital account liberalization have to a large extent lost autonomy over their exchange rate and monetary policies, which in turn has severely limited their capacity to implement countercyclical macroeconomic policies (Ocampo, 2002a).

Problems of incomplete information and information failure have prevented deregulated financial systems from operating effectively and have led lenders to finance unsound investments, misallocating valuable resources. The prominence of short-term speculative flows within these systems has decreased the availability of resources for productive investment and created new constraints to development policy.

Some of the crises that have occurred in connection with major economic developments have produced severe economic and social losses. A study of countries that experienced financial crises between 1975 and 1994 showed that national GDP growth declined by an average of 1.3 per cent over the five years immediately following the respective crises (Stiglitz, 1998).

Economic crises have also raised levels of inequality within countries. During such crises, job scarcity reduces the demand for labour, which drives down wages, especially among unskilled workers. These circumstances lead to increased inequality both in earnings and more generally, especially in countries in which the wage declines have been substantial and in which social protection systems have not yet been developed. This has been empirically demonstrated in different studies that have analysed the effects of financial crises on wage inequality in over 60 countries since the 1970s. For example, wage inequality increased in 62 and 73 per cent of the countries in Asia and Latin America, respectively, following their financial crises; however, no such post-crisis impact was evident in developed countries such as Finland, Norway and Spain (Diwan, 1999; Galbraith and Jiaqing, 1999).

The liberalization of financial and capital markets has led to substantial foreign direct investment (FDI). The effects of FDI on employment and growth have been mixed (International Labour Organization, 2004). Such investment has benefited certain countries, with the transfer of technology and know-how contributing to economic development. However, these countries already had a number of important conditions in place, including a certain level of education among wide sectors of the population, training institutions and some level of technological development to support the investments, and the existence of local firms able to absorb and benefit from the technology and skills transferred. Countries without such conditions, in which the links between FDI and the local economy have been weak, have benefited little from such investment. While the flow of investment capital into developing countries has increased overall, FDI remains highly concentrated in particular areas, further exacerbating inequalities between countries (International Labour Organization, 2004).

Trade liberalization

As mentioned previously, liberalization policies and market reforms have produced many asymmetries. In the case of trade liberalization, the transformation of the General Agreement on Tariffs and Trade (GATT) into the WTO has been crucial, broadening the scope of international trade negotiations and regulations beyond the reduction of tariffs and other direct barriers to trade in manufactures. Many other issues viewed as impediments to the free flow of goods and services between countries have come under the purview of the WTO. An important consideration in the present context is that WTO rules place restrictions on national policies, including social policies, if they are judged to be inconsistent with the provisions of WTO agreements. Any party, whether it be a country or a private interest or enterprise, can use the WTO dispute settlement mechanisms to challenge the local and national laws and regulations of another member country (Guimarães, 2004).

Even the staunchest advocates of the market economy agree that trade liberalization does not ensure that all actors will prosper without support either directly from the State or through some form of regulation, particularly in emerging economies (Lowi, 2001). One of the more difficult challenges linked to the inequalities characterizing the new international trade regime is the undue primacy given to free trade to the detriment of the long-term sustainability of economic growth and social development.

Research suggests that the proliferation of free trade agreements may further widen inequality between countries (World Bank, 2004a). A World Bank study estimates that a broad global trade agreement could increase world income by US$ 263 billion by 2015, with the developing country share amounting to US$ 109 billion. However, if all developing countries had bilateral agreements with the largest trading partners, namely the EU, the United States, Canada and Japan, global income would rise by just US$ 112 billion, or less than half the previous estimate. Further, this US$ 112 billion increase would derive from a US$ 133 billion rise in income among the wealthiest countries and a corresponding loss of US$ 21 billion among developing countries (World Bank, 2004a).

The relationship between trade liberalization and poverty eradication has recently been subjected to close scrutiny by both international organizations and academia. UNCTAD, for example, examined the trade liberalization experiences of 66 developing countries over five-year periods (1990-1995 or 1995-2000) and concluded that the relationship between trade liberalization and poverty reduction was neither automatic nor straightforward.[2] Similarly, a review of relevant academic studies found no simple general conclusion about the relationship between the two (Copeland and Taylor, 2004). UNCTAD did indicate, however, that countries that had opened up more gradually tended to exhibit a better trade-poverty relationship than did those that had opened up furthest and fastest and those that had retained the most trade restrictions against other countries.

The empirical literature on trade liberalization in Africa identifies various channels through which trade has impacted the continent in terms of investment composition, household welfare, income distribution and the competitiveness of local firms (Geda, 2004). Most cross-country regressions show that openness is positively correlated with income inequality (see, for example, Spilimbergo, Londoño and Skezely, 1999; Fischer, 2000).

In industrialized countries, trade and financial liberalization have contributed to the widening of within-country inequalities. The transfer of industries to lower-cost countries has pushed down the salaries of those engaged in low-skilled work in the more traditional manufacturing industries and has reduced the availability of these types of jobs in developed countries. In recent years, this phenomenon has begun to affect other types of jobs as well, including those in the high-technology sector.

Trade liberalization policies have affected the prospects for poverty reduction in both developed and developing countries. As roughly three quarters of the poor live in rural areas, poverty cannot be reduced in most of the developing world unless agricultural productivity is characterized by sustained growth. The deterioration of already low agricultural incomes is a major factor in the perpetuation of rural poverty. While the decline in the prices of agricultural goods may reduce the cost of consumption for poor people, it also means lower incomes for farmers and a reduction in their demand for other goods and services in rural areas.

Protectionist practices and agricultural subsidies in developed countries are recognized as major factors contributing to low agricultural production and incomes in the developing world. While imports from other developed countries are subject to an average tariff rate of 1 per cent, agricultural products from developing countries are taxed at 9 per cent by the United States and 20 per cent by the EU, and textile levies average 8.9 and 7.9 per cent, respectively. This asymmetry is vividly reflected in the trade situation of Latin America and the Caribbean. The region imposes an 8.5 per cent duty on non-agricultural imports (mostly from industrialized countries), but its own agricultural products are subject to a 20.4 per cent duty when exported to industrialized countries. Overall, developing countries lose in excess of US$ 40 billion annually from agricultural exports due to the imposition of import duties by developed countries. This amount is equivalent to a significant proportion of the projected financial requirements for the successful achievement of the Millennium Development Goals (Guadagni, 2004).

Financing the social agenda

Financing is a crucial element for the new context for social development, and for the concerted national and international efforts to reverse present inequalities within and between countries. While the provision of financial resources alone does not automatically guarantee positive results, such resources are nonetheless a prerequisite for social development. There has been ample discussion of possible ways to finance social development, with many countries undertaking commitments to increase the levels and quality of ODA. Increased attention is also being directed towards the issues of migrant remittances and domestic financing, as well as ways to invest the peace dividend in social development.

Figure V.1. Aid from all Development Assistance Committee (DAC) donors as a percentage of gross domestic product: the long-term trend to 2004

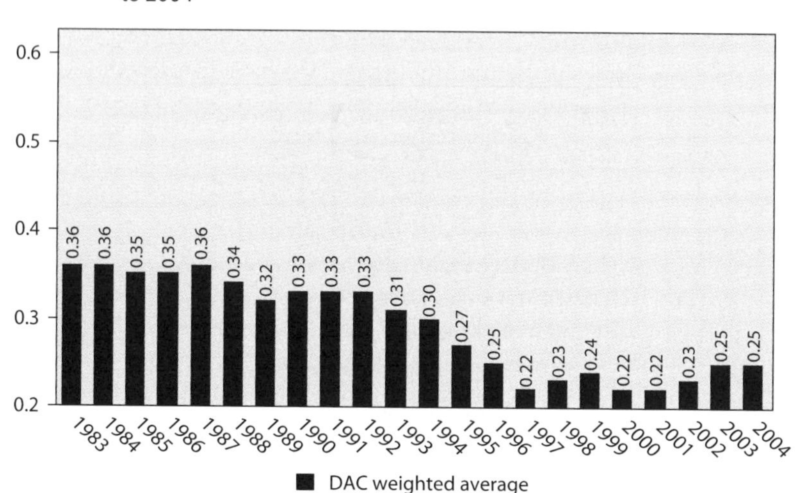

Source: iDevelopment Initiatives, "Briefing on Aid in 2004" (www.devinit.org/dagfigs2004brief2.pdf.; accessed 20 May 2005).

Official development assistance

The International Conference on Financing for Development was held in Monterrey, Mexico, from 18 to 22 March 2002. In the Monterrey Consensus adopted at the Conference, heads of State and Government pledged to undertake actions to improve financing for development. The Conference marked the first quadripartite exchange of views between Governments, civil society, the business community and institutional stakeholders on global economic issues.

As a component of efforts to mobilize international assistance, repeated calls have been made for raising current levels of ODA as soon as possible to increase the flow of resources available for social development. As a share of the combined GNI of the 22 Development Assistance Committee (DAC) donors, the overall level of ODA decreased from 0.36 per cent in 1987 to 0.22 per cent in 2001. Although ODA has recently begun to climb, rising to 0.25 per cent in 2004 from its lowest point in the late 1990s (see figure V.1), it is still far below the internationally agreed target of 0.7 per cent called for by the General Assembly 35 years ago (Organisation for Economic Cooperation and Development, 2005a).

Only Norway, Denmark, Sweden, Luxembourg and the Netherlands have met and surpassed the United Nations ODA target of 0.7 per cent. Figures for 2004 indicate a large gap between these five countries and the other 17 DAC donor countries (with the exception of Portugal, which is close to

Figure V.2. Aid from Development Assistance Committee (DAC) donors as a proportion of gross domestic product[a]

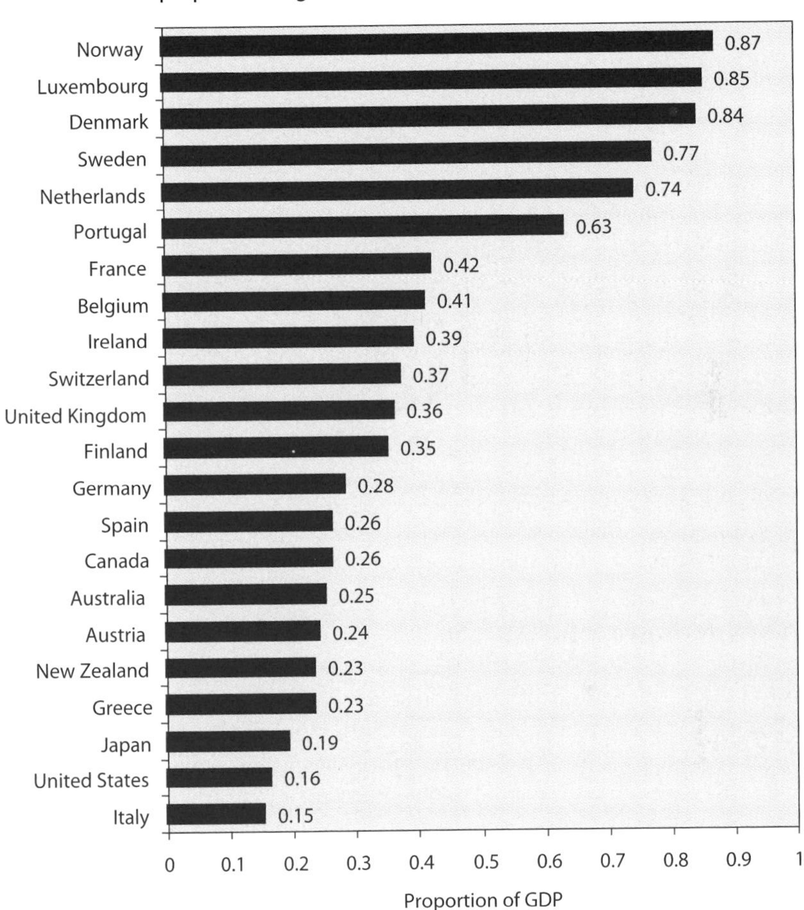

Source: iDevelopment Initiatives, "Briefing on Aid in 2004" (www.devinit.org/dagfigs2004brief2.pdf.; accessed 20 May 2005).

a Preliminary data obtained on 11 April 2005.

meeting the target). As shown in figure V.2, most of the G-7 countries[3] allocated a much lower proportion of their gross national income to ODA than the United Nations target.

At the International Conference on Financing for Development, major aid donors pledged to increase levels of development assistance. If donors honour the commitments made in Monterrey, aid flows will rise to approximately US$ 88 billion by 2006, up from US$ 78.6 billion in 2004, the highest level of ODA to date (Organisation for Economic Cooperation and Development, 2005b). While these developments appear to represent a step in the right direction, the Secretary-General of the United Nations has emphasized that substantially greater increases in ODA are needed to reach the target of 0.7 per cent by 2015. Developed countries that have not already established timetables for expanding ODA are called upon to do so, starting with significant increases no later than 2006 and achieving a level of 0.5 per cent by 2009. Action must also be taken to increase the quality, transparency, accountability and predictability of ODA (United Nations, 2005c).

Aid flows tend to be volatile, which can compromise their effectiveness. ODA follows the rise and fall of economic cycles in donor countries and is affected by both shifts in donor policies and assessments of recipient country policies. A decline in aid generally leads to costly fiscal adjustments in the form of increased taxation and spending cuts, which reinforce the cyclical effect of diminishing aid. A surge in aid flows can create macroeconomic problems, especially in countries with underdeveloped financial sectors, which often have low absorptive capacities. Surges can cause exchange rate appreciation, which, when sustained, can lead to currency overvaluation (United Nations, 2005d).

ODA has generally been concentrated among a select group of countries. Because donors have tended to favour certain recipients, more than half of the net bilateral aid disbursed since the 1980s has been directed to just 20 countries. This concentration has evolved largely as a result of donor perceptions of aid efficiency (United Nations, 2005d).

Recent increases in ODA have been earmarked for expenditures on emergency aid, debt relief, technical assistance or aid to countries that donors deem critical for reasons of political or security, and this has effectively reduced the resources available to poor countries for social development (United Nations, 2005c). While emergency aid is important, it does not support long-term development and does not represent a real increase in developmental aid. For this reason, despite the recent increases in donor assistance, the effective contribution of ODA to development programme financing in recipient countries has been limited. In other words, even with the recent recovery in recorded donor contributions, ODA has been a declining source of budgetary resources for developing countries, limiting their capacity to pursue the Millennium Development Goals. In support of these Goals, the call for increased ODA must refer specifically to real cash increases (United Nations, 2005d).

Innovative sources of financing

New proposals are being considered for innovative development financing that complements existing ODA mechanisms and ensures greater predictability in the flow of development assistance. The five-year review of the 1995 World Summit for Social Development gave new impetus to the debate on alternative sources of development financing. A recent study has explored several potential options for development support, proposing both short- and longer-run mechanisms (Atkinson, 2004). Their adoption and implementation would depend, in part, on their feasibility and the consensus of the partners involved. One alternative is the International Finance Facility (IFF), a short-run mechanism that would frontload new long-term donor commitments by issuing bonds in international capital markets. This would substantially increase the development funds immediately available and lend aid flows greater stability and predictability. Another short-run mechanism is the use of special drawing rights (SDR) for development purposes. This instrument could potentially be utilized to supplement the existing official reserves of countries and provide emergency financing during crises.

Potential long-run financing mechanisms include a global lottery and global taxes, the revenues of which would be used for development. The suggested taxes on currency transactions, arms sales and the consumption of fuels producing greenhouse gases could generate enough funds to combat poverty and hunger worldwide. It is estimated that implementation of the currency transaction tax would generate between US$ 16.8 billion and US$ 35.4 billion in revenues per annum. A tax on the emission of greenhouse gases would provide a significant source of development financing while also discouraging harmful behaviour. Building on the 1992 United Nations Framework Convention on Climate Change, the imposition of a US$ 21-per-ton tax on greenhouse gas emissions could yield US$ 130 billion per year if applied globally and US$ 61 billion annually if applied only to wealthy countries. A tax on arms sales could generate between US$ 2.5 billion and US$ 8 billion annually while discouraging military spending (Atkinson, 2004).

Global taxation to finance development would have to be nationally mandated and internationally coordinated to prevent it from being perceived as an infringement on the fiscal sovereignty of participating countries. In applying global taxation, the creation of a new international bureaucracy should be avoided. Universal participation would not be required, though more widespread involvement would translate into higher levels of resources and would also reduce the risk of free-riding (Atkinson, 2004).

Arranging for migrant workers to remit their earnings through regulated financial institutions would provide another significant opportunity to accrue resources for development. By facilitating better access to banking institutions for foreign workers and obtaining the support of local financial institutions in recipient countries, joint efforts could be launched to further reduce remittance costs.

Migrant remittances

Globalization, liberalization and the growing integration of economies have meant that people, and not just jobs and capital, are moving across borders in greater numbers and with increasing frequency (United Nations, 2003b). Persistent and growing income inequalities between countries and widening demographic disparities, combined with the availability of cheaper and more accessible forms of transportation, have raised international migration flows to unprecedented levels. In 2000, an estimated 175 million people (or roughly 1 in 35) worldwide were living outside their countries of birth (United Nations, 2004d). A growing number of migrants are moving from developing to developed countries in search of jobs and better economic opportunities. At their destinations, migrants are often able to earn higher incomes and improve their standard of living. Migrant flows are high even within developing regions, where forced migration and heavy refugee movements often exert considerable pressure on limited resources.

Although many recent migrants have been admitted to a number of developed countries on the basis of family reunification (SOPEMI [Continuous Reporting System on Migration], 2003), international migration still occurs largely in response to perceived inequalities of opportunity between sending and receiving countries. Historically, migrant pools have often reflected a bias towards the more skilled segments of the population in the countries of origin; however, this trend is beginning to change in response to labour shortages and new labour demands in many developed countries. Several countries that seek to fill gaps in the supply of low-skilled labour tolerate undocumented migration and visa violations, though this is often not widely acknowledged by Governments (United Nations, 2004d).

The heavy outflow of migrants from developing countries has mixed economic and social repercussions in both sending and receiving communities. In the countries of origin, emigration often depletes an already limited skilled labour force, making the benefits of economic reform even more difficult to realize. Fiscal revenue from taxation may also decline, as migrants are more likely to be among the highest income earners. On the positive side, emigration releases jobs in the countries of origin and may provide opportunities for those previously unemployed (United Nations, 2004d).

Migrant earnings constitute a considerable and growing source of remittance flows to labour-sending countries, in spite of the sometimes precarious economic situation of foreign workers in various host countries. Data on remittances are incomplete and almost certainly underestimate the flows of funds through informal channels. Nonetheless, available data suggest that remittances totalled US$ 130 billion in 2002, with US$ 79 billion going to developing countries. For a growing number of countries, remittances have surpassed ODA in volume and now constitute the second largest source of financial flows after FDI (United Nations, 2004d).

Remittances to developing countries tend to be concentrated in particular regions. The largest amounts go to Latin America and the Caribbean, followed by Eastern and Southern Asia, while sub-Saharan Africa receives only 1.5 per cent of the total. The European Union accounts for the largest source of remittance payments, followed by the United States and countries in the Middle East (United Nations, 2004d).

There is a positive statistical correlation between remittances and poverty reduction; "on average, a 10 per cent increase in the share of international remittances in a country's GDP will lead to a 1.6 per cent decline in the share of people living in poverty" (Adams and Page, 2003). International migration, per se, has also been shown to have a strong statistical impact on reducing poverty; a 10 per cent rise in the proportion of international migrants in a country's population is associated with a 1.9 per cent decline in the share of people living on less than US$ 1 per day.

The deployment of workers' remittances and the impact they may have on families and communities are receiving considerable attention. By and large, migrants appear to use their incomes "wisely", with the benefits generally outweighing the costs of migrating. Remittances tend to be used primarily for consumption rather than investment. However, they are also frequently utilized to pay for the education of children and youth or to improve the quality of housing, which are clearly investments. Even when remittances are spent on consumption, they have an indirect effect on the community, as consumption stimulates local economic growth (Skeldon, 2002). Growing attention has been given to the possibility of using remittances to "bank" the poor at the sending and receiving ends, channelling the funds towards more productive uses such as the financing of small and micro enterprises or the adoption of financial savings and other investment strategies for both migrant and recipient households.

It is difficult to measure the impact of remittances on inequality. Remittances may intensify financial and social inequalities, as those who migrate tend to come from the "wealthier" families in a community. Overall, however, the findings have been mixed. For example, a study in Pakistan found that inequalities had intensified between migrant and non-migrant households, but also found that the distribution of remittances was spread over a relatively wide range of groups and areas. A study in Thailand has indicated that remittances to poor households may have a much greater relative impact on poverty alleviation, even though the per capita amounts are much lower than those sent to wealthier families (Skeldon, 2002).

The economic impact on migrants' families is often significant, and those who do not migrate may experience envy and growing resentment as they witness the effects of remittances on the households of migrants. According to a study of migration in India, such resentment contributed to an outbreak of violent conflict in which non-migrant households railed against the visible signs of affluence made possible by emigrants' earnings (Allen, 2003). Sustaining the positive contributions of remittances will require proper management and recognition of the feelings of resentment and exclusion among non-migrant families. Clearly, the impact of migration and remittances on sending and receiving countries is different, with the social costs and benefits also varying at the community and national levels.

Figure V.3. Social sector spending among country groupings classified by income

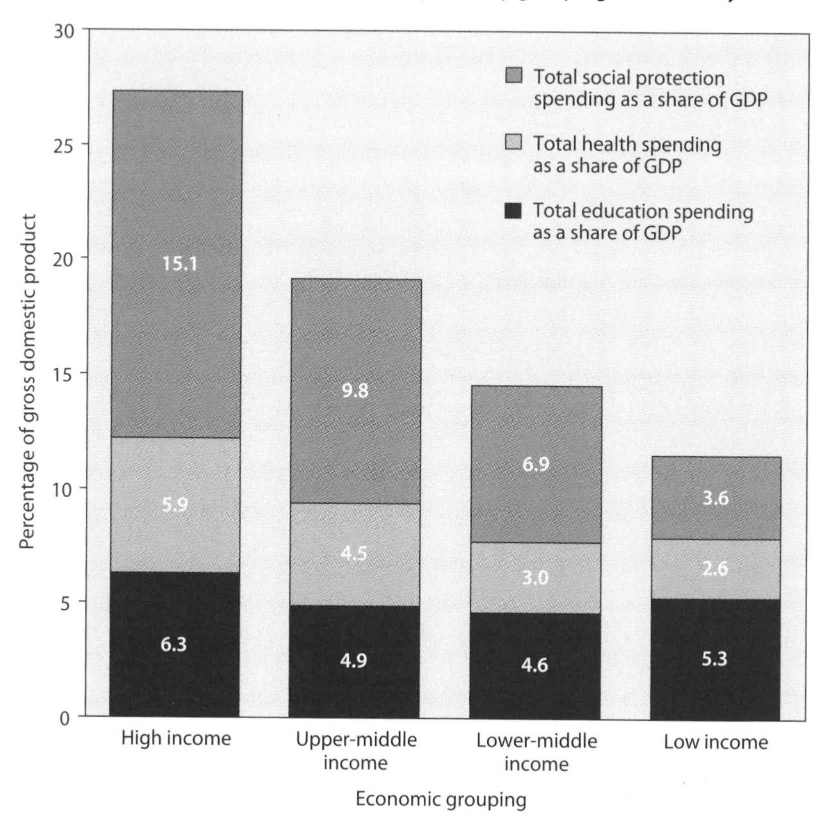

Source: P. Kelly and V. Saiz-Omeñaca, "The allocation of government expenditure in the world, 1990-2001", unpublished paper (New York, United Nations, Department of Economic and Social Affairs, Division for Social Policy and Development, November 2004).

Domestic financing

With the implementation of liberalization policies, measures with a direct impact on the reduction of inequalities, such as progressive taxation and changes in the level and composition of public expenditure, have become less redistributive in many countries. A survey of 36 developing and transition economies indicated, for example, that during the 1980s and 1990s overall tax progressivity and the share of direct taxes in total taxes declined, and the ratio of taxes to GDP fell by one percentage point on average (Chu, Davoodi and Gupta, 2000). Tax changes in Latin America effectively shifted the burden of taxation from the wealthy to the middle- and lower-income segments of society (Morley, 2000). In OECD countries in which liberalization policies have been most consistently implemented, there have been reductions in expenditures on universal social programmes, resulting in lower transfers from the public budget to low-income households (Weeks, 2004).

In many cases, public finance reforms have transferred responsibility for social sector financing and oversight from the public sector to the private sector. This shift is most visible in the provision of social services in a number of developing countries, where services traditionally provided by the public sector at subsidized rates have in some cases been privatized or outsourced to private contractors. The new orthodoxy favours cost recovery and a fee-for-service approach, which has placed many services beyond the reach of the poor. The introduction of user fees for health care and education has resulted in greater social exclusion, with reduced social assistance and scaled-down public health programmes. The increase in non-economic inequalities in areas such as education and health care both within and between countries is highly correlated with these factors.

The rise in non-economic inequalities is also partially attributable to the higher government priority given to spending on areas such as economic affairs and defence than to spending on health, education, social protection and other social sector programmes. A recent study has attempted to identify how Governments allocate their resources, focusing on the distribution of resources between the social sectors and other areas of priority and on the impact public spending patterns have on social development (Kelly and Saiz-Omeñaca, 2004).

Research findings point to wide disparities in social sector spending between different groups of countries classified according to their level of economic development. High-income countries spend an average of 27 per cent of GDP on the social sectors, compared with 19 and 15 per cent respectively in upper-middle- and lower-middle-income countries and 12 per cent in low-income countries (Kelly and Saiz-Omeñaca, 2004). Overall, rich countries devote an average of two and a half times more of their national wealth to the health, education and welfare of their citizens than do poor countries (see figure V.3).

Among the social sectors, the greatest variation in spending as a share of GDP is found in the area of social protection, followed by health and, to a lesser degree, education. On average, high-income countries funnel 15 per cent of their GDP into various forms of social protection such as pensions, unemployment and disability benefits, and accident and medical insurance, while upper-middle-income countries allocate 10 per cent and lower-middle-income countries 7 per cent. Most strikingly, low-income countries allocate less than 4 per cent of GDP to social protection, or about one quarter of the share spent by high-income countries.

Health spending also varies significantly among economic groupings. High-income countries spend an average of 6 per cent of their GDP on health, or more than double the 3 per cent allocated by low-income countries. Considering the importance of health to people's well-being, not to

Figure V.4. Defence and social sector spending in countries with the highest defence expenditures

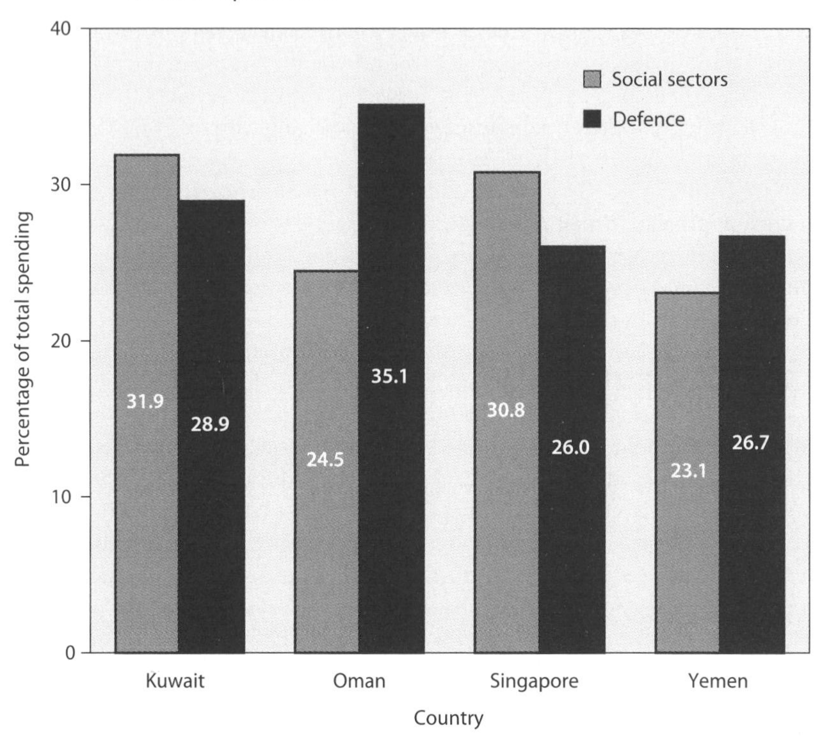

Source: P. Kelly and V. Saiz-Omeñaca, "The allocation of government expenditure in the world, 1990-2001", unpublished paper (New York, United Nations, Department of Economic and Social Affairs, Division for Social Policy and Development, November 2004).

mention its link to poverty reduction, the low level of resources invested in health care by poorer countries is especially troubling.

Education constitutes the one bright spot among the social sectors in terms of relative proportions of State spending. Although high-income countries still allocate more of their GDP to education (6.3 per cent, versus 5.3 per cent among lower-income countries), the difference is far less pronounced than in the social protection and health sectors. Moreover, low-income countries actually spend a higher proportion of their GDP on education than do lower-middle- or upper-middle-income countries. The importance attached to education by many lower-income countries is laudable, and the trend towards investment in education should continue. However, education alone is not enough to reduce poverty and improve living standards. Adequate investment should be made in all the social sectors, including health and social protection, in order to achieve marked improvements in social development.

The financing of social sector programmes is directly related to the collection of taxes, the primary component of the State resource base. Rather

Figure V.5. Defence and social spending in countries with the highest social sector expenditures

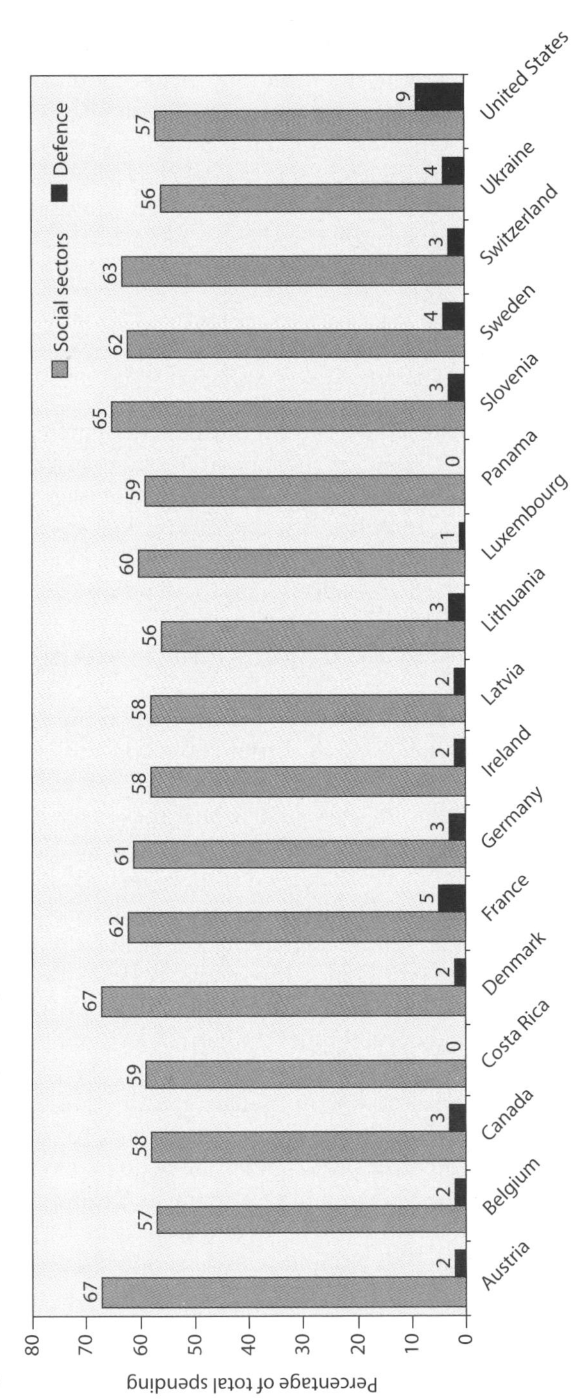

Source: P. Kelly and V. Saiz-Omeñaca, "The allocation of government expenditure in the world, 1990-2001", unpublished paper (New York, United Nations, Department of Economic and Social Affairs, Division for Social Policy and Development, November 2004).

than raising taxes to provide additional funding for social programmes, many Governments have felt compelled to lower average corporate tax rates in order to attract and retain FDI; among the world's 30 richest countries, the average rate of corporate tax fell from 37.6 per cent in 1996 to 30.8 per cent in 2003 (International Labour Organization, 2004). A similar phenomenon can be seen in the taxation of high-income earners, who are also relatively more mobile. In many cases, to compensate for these tax cuts, Governments have gradually increased their dependence on indirect taxes such as sales taxes (especially the value added tax, or VAT) and taxes on relatively immobile (or less mobile) factors such as labour.

The peace dividend

Financing for development would also benefit from reductions in military expenditures, as the freed-up public resources could be redirected to investment in social development. According to a recent study of worldwide government spending over a 10-year period, countries that dedicated a higher share of total public expenditure to the defence sector tended to be among those that allocated the lowest portion of the State budget to the social sectors (see figure V.4). Likewise, as shown in figure V.5, countries with the highest levels of social sector spending were found to have the lowest defence spending (Kelly and Saiz-Omeñaca, 2004).

Over the past several years, the reallocation of resources from defence to social development has not taken place. Estimated world military expenditures[4] declined for five straight years, falling from US$ 762 billion in 1993 to a low of US$ 690 billion in 1998, after which they began to rise (Stockholm International Peace Research Institute, 2003; United Nations, 2004b). By 2002, defence spending had increased to an estimated US$ 784 billion, surpassing the 1993 level for the first time. World military expenditures reached US$ 956 billion in 2003, representing 2.6 per cent of global GNP (United Nations, 2004b; Stockholm International Peace Research Institute, 2004), and will probably exceed US$ 1 trillion in 2005 (United Nations, 2005b). This figure is almost 20 times the current level of development aid.

As indicated above, the global decline in military spending during the 1990s has been dramatically reversed. These figures stand in sharp contrast to the current levels of ODA and those projected for the period 2006-2010. It has been asserted that all of the Millennium Development Goals could be met in developing countries by 2015 if ODA were increased by US$ 150 billion (United Nations, 2005d). This amount represents only a fraction of the more than US$ 900 billion the world is now spending in a single year on arms and other means of destruction (United Nations Millennium Project, 2005). The reallocation of defence-related expenditures to social development requires the concerted action of the international community, with the aim of realizing the double dividend of sufficient funding for social programmes and the reduction of armed conflict and violence.

The role of the State and civil society

The trend towards economic liberalization that characterized the 1980s and 1990s provoked a reaction to ensure that the social dimension was taken into account in economic and structural adjustment policies. This response is largely a consequence of the appeals by civil society and NGOs, which have seen their numbers and influence rise substantially over the decades. Civil society activism has also helped promote greater self-awareness of rights and awareness of the relative inequality between people, which has been bolstered in recent years by the growing interest in human rights and increased access to information on a global scale.

The last decade has witnessed growing interest in improving the status of various social groups, as evidenced by the considerable attention given to the rights of indigenous peoples and persons with disabilities and to poverty among older persons and unemployment among youth; however, there has been less interest shown in developing policies to equalize the distribution of income and wealth. The focus of many political struggles has shifted away from the latter to other kinds of differences and inequalities, especially those based on race and gender, with particular attention given to political and civil rights.

There has been a very important shift in the past two decades in the way individuals and social groups have chosen to be represented and defend their interests nationally and internationally. Through the last decade of the twentieth century, "trade unions represented civil society interests, not only on issues such as employment and wages, but also on many other issues related to social development, such as pensions, health care and social protection. The trade unions appear to have been affected by the long-term trend of declining relative size in union membership, as measured by union 'density rates'—the percentage of workers who belong to unions" (International Labour Organization, 1997).

As the role of trade unions in social activism has declined, other types of civil society organizations and non-profit groups have flourished. The social environment has favoured non-governmental actors and has supported the growing trend towards partnership in fulfilling many of the responsibilities hitherto carried out solely by State. The participation of civil society organizations in the national and international arenas has become crucial, as these entities defend the interests of groups whose voices might otherwise never be heard. Starting with their active participation in the major world conferences of the 1990s, civil society organizations "have articulated new ideas and proposals, argued and negotiated, protested and exercised political pressure" (Cardoso, 2004), and in so doing have created an unprecedented new international public space.

The contribution of religious organizations should not be underestimated. Traditionally, these organizations have played an important role in social development, mainly through the direct provision of social services in areas such as health and education. In some countries, the involvement of religious and/or other civil society organizations in service delivery has been of such magnitude that these countries have been able to resist the wave of privatization driven by market reforms in recent decades. Religious organizations have expanded their role to include greater advocacy and have acquired a more directly political voice. These groups are much more inclined now than in the past to assume an active role in the international debate and to try to influence significant decisions in the social arena. Their scope of activity now encompasses not only education and health, but also the environment, human rights and democratic governance.

International organizations and even private voluntary concerns have recently begun to establish their own labour standards and environmental rules, and while this trend is welcome, it is also believed to represent a response to the possible impact of an apparent "race to the bottom", during which market forces are left unchecked. The Global Compact, launched in July 2000, and the Equator Principles, drafted in October 2002 and adopted by a growing number of major investment banks since then, are noteworthy among the voluntary schemes that, by virtue of their emergence, lend credence to the notion that a "race to the bottom" has occurred and corroborate the need for initiatives to counter the tendency.

The Global Compact's 10 universal principles on human rights, labour, the environment and anti-corruption, which are meant to inspire more responsible and sustainable business practices, reflect a growing consensus and a coming together of United Nations agencies, labour and civil society organizations, and corporate interests. It is important to note that these commitments, while welcome, represent a set of *promises*, as there is no enforcement mechanism to hold private-sector actors accountable for adhering to the principles of the Global Compact. The 17 Equator Principles are intended to serve as a common framework for assessing and addressing environmental and social risks in project financing, and for the implementation of relevant procedures and standards across all industry sectors globally (Equator Principles, 2004). The overall framework derives from policies and guidelines established by the World Bank and the International Finance Corporation (Equator Principles, 2004). The Equator Principles have been adopted by a number of organizations, and it is estimated that the 23 banks among the 25 financial institutions applying the Principles approved US$ 55.1 billion in project loans in 2003, representing 75 per cent of the US$ 73.5 billion in project loans approved by this group of banks that year (Dealogic, 2004).

It should be emphasized that the relative decline in some traditional forms of societal representation and the emergence of other non-State actors do not presuppose the further weakening of the State. In recent years it has been increasingly recognized, in spite of the ideological swings of the past decade, "that the State still holds key responsibilities in regulatory matters and in its role of articulating diverse productive, community and social sectors" (Cardoso, 1995; World Bank, 1997; United Nations, 2004c, para. 47).

In line with the structural adjustment and transition policies implemented over more than a decade, there emerged a growing tendency to reduce the role of the State; however, in the late 1990s, this trend began to reverse itself as country experiences demonstrated the folly of privatizing State functions on a large scale. Gradually, a consensus has evolved that the State plays an important role in social and economic development and that its functions cannot be completely taken over by the private sector or executed within the framework of public/private or public/civil-society partnerships.

In the current approaches to development it is acknowledged that public regulation and State-led policies still represent contributions to the development process that are unique, necessary and indispensable (Guimarães, 1996). The essential importance of the State transcends the logic of market forces, particularly in areas such as ethics, equality, social justice and the defence of rights intrinsic to citizenship, which are foreign to market mechanisms and institutions. The State role is necessary because the very logic of capital accumulation requires the provision of "public goods" and "merit goods" that either cannot be spontaneously produced in the market or can only be produced in suboptimal quantities.[5] The State is also more effective in addressing risk, vulnerability, social exclusion, destitution and many other issues not amenable to microeconomic calculus, particularly when future generations (who, by definition, do not participate in today's market) are brought into consideration.

While it is recognized that the separate and combined functions of governmental and non-governmental actors are essential, the manner in which they carry out these functions is equally critical. Over the past two decades, the changes in the roles and functions of the State and civil society and the respective approaches they have adopted have not always been favourable to the reduction of inequality and the pursuit of social justice. While the renewed recognition of the necessary involvement of the State in promoting development and poverty eradication is a welcome reversal of the earlier trend towards minimizing the State's role in ensuring social justice, little has been done to instigate progressive taxation and other redistributive measures in order to reduce inequality. Likewise, while equal political and civil rights for vulnerable and marginalized groups have been placed on the public agenda largely as a consequence of the growing numbers and rising influence of civil society organizations, the focus of advocacy appears to be shifting away from the equitable distribution of income and assets towards more general political and civil rights. This state of affairs represents the political and institutional framework in which issues of inequality are considered today.

Conclusion

As stated in the Millennium Declaration, "the central challenge we face today is to ensure that globalization becomes a positive force for all the world's people. For while globalization offers great opportunities, at present its benefits are very unevenly shared, while its costs are unevenly distributed. ... [O]nly through broad and sustained efforts to create a shared future, based upon our common humanity in all its diversity, can globalization be made fully inclusive and equitable" (United Nations, 2000, para. 5).

It is in this context that efforts must be undertaken to ensure that market-driven reforms, the multilateral trading system embodied by the WTO, and other aspects or components of the international economy do not interfere with the possibilities for realizing the progressively redistributive dimensions of social development. Actively pursuing such possibilities not only represents a requirement for reducing poverty and inequality, promoting employment and fostering social integration (the major priorities on the social development agenda today), but also constitutes a moral and ethical imperative.

In the context of development, the quantity of growth (the simple increment of material output or economic growth) has remained the primary focus. It is becoming increasingly apparent, however, that the single most important challenge facing the world in this new millennium is enhancing the quality of growth (increasing levels of well-being and reducing socio-economic inequalities). In acknowledgement of this fact, measures to foster sustainable economic growth "must be accompanied by indispensable distributive policies and corrective and compensatory policies to redress the injustices and imbalances of the past" (Ricupero, 2001).

National, regional and international efforts should be aimed at strengthening global governance and mechanisms to promote a more balanced and inclusive globalization. As the Secretary-General of the United Nations has stated, "millions of people around the world experience it [globalization] not as an agent of progress but as a disruptive and even destructive force, while many more millions are completely excluded from its benefits" (Grumberg and Khan, 2000).

While the main engine of globalization is "technology and the expansion and integration of markets, it is not a force of nature but the result of processes driven by human beings. Thus, globalization needs to be controlled so that it can be put at the service of humanity, which means that it needs to be carefully administered, by sovereign countries at the national level, and through multilateral cooperation at the international level" (Grumberg and Khan, 2000). Adequate management of the multifaceted processes associated with the current wave of globalization is required; more to the point, "open-minded, tolerant and pragmatic approaches to the development challenge, consistent with today's increasingly interdependent world, are urgently needed to place economic policy once again at the service of social justice and stability" (United Nations Conference on Trade and Development, 2003).

Notes

1 It should be noted, however, that there are instances in which, as a result of pressure from civil society organizations (in particular those in developed countries), multinationals have begun to promote higher social and environmental standards.

2 Among these 66 countries, 51 succeeded in increasing exports over the five-year period. Further analysis of the average private per capita consumption of these 51 countries indicated that 22 of them (less than half) had experienced the "virtuous trade effect", meaning that average private per capita consumption had increased with export expansion during the five-year period examined; 11 had experienced an ambiguous trade effect; and 18 had experienced an immiserizing trade effect, meaning that average private per capita consumption had decreased with export expansion (see UNCTAD, 2004a, p. 10).

3 The Group of Seven major industrialized countries (G-7) includes Canada, France, Germany, Italy, Japan, the United Kingdom and the United States.

4 Measured in constant 2000 United States dollars and at market exchange rates.

5 "Merit goods", often mentioned in the literature on welfare economics, are also referred to as "goods of social value". The concept of "public goods" focuses on the interdependence of consumers and other economic agents, whereas the notion of merit goods, or goods of social value, emphasizes the decision of society to provide certain goods to all citizens. Although the differentiation between these concepts is appropriate in the context of welfare economics, the common use of the term "public goods" in social and political analysis typically encompasses both (see José Antonio Ocampo, 2005, pp. 11-20).

Chapter VI
The way forward: policies to reduce inequality[1]

The present *Report* has endeavoured to make a strong case for focusing on the inequality predicament, a situation that jeopardizes the quest for social justice and social development—the very same quest that led world leaders to gather at the World Summit for Social Development in Copenhagen 10 years ago and commit themselves to specific actions to bring about the social betterment of humanity.

Addressing the inequality predicament requires a multifaceted normative and policy approach that puts human beings at the centre of development, one that considers economic growth as a means and not as an end in itself—an approach for which the ultimate goal is to increase, protect and attain improvements in the quality of life of current and future generations. The approach should be socially sustainable in reducing poverty and inequality and in promoting social justice. It should be culturally sustainable, conserving values, practices and symbols of identity that determine social cohesion and national identity over time. It should be politically sustainable, deepening democracy, transparency and accountability, and thereby guaranteeing the access to and participation of all sectors of society in public decision-making. Finally, the approach should be environmentally sustainable, taking into account access to and use of natural resources and the preservation of biodiversity.

This approach is based on the fact that social development and economic development are two sides of the same coin. They are equally important and mutually reinforcing; one cannot be achieved without the other. Societies that do not provide educational opportunities for all, adequate health care and decent employment are doomed to fail. Countries in which the needs and rights of future generations are not considered, in which women do not enjoy the same rights as men and in which social disintegration is rife will not achieve sustainable economic development. There are countless examples of such societies, both present and past. There is an urgent need to create an environment in which a multitude of positive examples can be provided in the future—one in which a holistic view of development prevails.

The comprehensive vision of social development agreed upon at the World Summit for Social Development in Copenhagen in 1995 and reaffirmed in Geneva in 2000 and in New York in 2005 has yet to receive the attention it deserves. The enabling environment envisaged by the Copenh-gen Declaration was conceived so as to create the conditions for pe[illegible] achieve social development. The economic, political, social, legal a[illegible] dimensions embedded in it are especially important. The commitments on eradicating poverty, promotion of full employment and social integration were accompanied by far-reaching policy recommendations based on the axiom that the well-being of people should be the centrepiece of national and international public attention.[2] Its implementation ought to dominate and shape the agendas of national Governments and international organizations in order to achieve sustainable social and economic development and foster the achievement of the Millennium Development Goals.

Redressing global asymmetries

The imbalance between the pace of globalization and the prevailing regulatory framework has produced many asymmetries requiring correction. At the political and institutional levels, emphasis should be placed on the equitable distribution of the benefits in an increasingly open world economy, with actions that promote democratic participation by all countries and peoples in the decision-making processes that govern international relations. Implementing people-centred development requires an approach that places the highest priority on the long-term objectives of social development. These overarching policy goals require the following:

- That actions are taken by the international community to lend political and institutional support to national capacity-building in the developing world, particularly to restoring the regulatory capacity of public institutions and especially in areas where privatization of the delivery of social services has created new challenges to and difficulties in the actual exercise of individual and collective rights to education, health and other social rights of citizenship;
- That a necessary balance is established between market forces and the public interest, especially through appropriate State regulation and oversight of corporate power and market forces;
- That flexibility is introduced into macroeconomic policies in order for national policies to counter the negative impacts of globalization on social development. Such an undertaking entails mainstreaming employment and poverty objectives into short-term macroeconomic policies and structural adjustment programmes. This step is particularly important in view of the constraints arising from competitive pressures brought about by international trade. Specific measures should also be introduced in foreign direct investment to promote domestic productive linkages and job creation;
- That a global minimum standard is established for social protection in order to stabilize incomes, distribute the gains of globalization for the benefit of all and support the development of new capabilities. The international standard, built on and harmonizing all the initiatives analysed

in the present *Report*, would prevent the "race to the bottom" in which countries are forced to overlook or limit social rules and regulations in order to remain competitive in the international market;

- That proposals for the reform of global financial architecture translate into action, particularly by increasing the surveillance and regulation of international capital flows providing adequate room to manoeuvre for the counter-cyclical macroeconomic policies of developing countries; and by strengthening regional cooperation efforts;
- That the various international social and economic regimes are reoriented towards a more coherent and integrated approach, with special attention given to the harmonization of relevant WTO agreements with other multilateral agreements in the social arena;
- That innovative ideas guaranteeing sufficient and stable financing to achieve major international development objectives are introduced to generate new sources of finance for development. The General Assembly and the Bretton Woods institutions should, in that regard, take the political decisions to advance some of the proposals that are under consideration.

Restructuring the social sector to promote equality and social integration requires political will, an effective State, and sufficient financial resources. To support this process it may be necessary to provide assistance aimed at strengthening the managerial, administrative and financial capacities of the State (United Nations, 2003a). The principal objective of such a strategy should be the democratization of the public education system through improvements in the coverage and quality of the primary and secondary levels within that system.

Suggested taxes on currency transactions, arms sales and the consumption of fuels producing greenhouse gases could generate enough funds to combat hunger and poverty worldwide. Other initiatives could include the proposed International Finance Facility (IFF), the use of special drawing rights (SDR)[3] and the creation of a lottery whose revenues would be used for development aid. In addition, the transfer costs of remittances should be reduced (Atkinson, 2004).

Intensifying integrated strategies and policies for poverty eradication

As a fundamental principle, policy decisions aimed at poverty reduction and eradication should be structured in such a way that these issues are addressed directly, instead of simply assuming that the trickle-down effects of other policies promote economic growth and development. Towards that end, specific policies and actions must be implemented to guarantee that the dimensions of equality are explicitly incorporated in policies and programmes designed to achieve poverty reduction; they must be complemented by specific measures to guarantee access by marginalized groups to assets and opportunities in general, and in particular to education, land, capital and technology.

Many aspects of social development, including poverty, gender equality, education and health, are addressed in the Millennium Development Goals and have therefore received increased global attention. However, the Goals, despite their galvanizing effect, are not a substitute for the much broader social development agenda. The international goal of halving the number of people living on less than US$ 1 a day by 2015 has become a universally recognized benchmark for evaluating development progress. Nonetheless, poverty alleviation strategies require a holistic approach that includes addressing inequalities, both within and between countries, in opportunities and access to resources, as well as promoting decent work. In support of this notion, it was stressed at the 10-year review of the World Summit for Social Development that the Millennium Declaration and the Copenhagen Declaration should be considered *mutually reinforcing* (United Nations, 2005a).

The gap between Africa and the rest of the world remains and has even widened in some respects. The marginalization of Africa in a globalizing world and the human suffering associated with a lack of development in the region are unacceptable.

Foremost among the key areas of international action is the commitment that technical and financial assistance will be earmarked in explicit quantitative targets to guarantee, within the framework of the New Partnership for Africa's Development, a favourable environment for social and economic development in Africa.

National institutions for social development need to be strengthened. To further this goal, it is necessary to include institution-building in development and poverty reduction strategies, including PRSPs. Increased emphasis must be placed on national ownership of the PRSPs; the policy formulation and development process should also involve civil society more effectively.

Most policy prescriptions are still developed and implemented largely without adequate analysis of how they affect the poorest and most vulnerable in society. In many countries, these groups still find themselves excluded from the planning processes and concrete actions designed to alleviate their plight. Efforts must be made to include the excluded and chronically poor in the consultative and participatory processes that accompany the development and review of poverty programmes.

Guaranteeing employment opportunities for all

The Secretary-General of the United Nations has stated that "the best antipoverty programme is employment. And the best road to economic empowerment and social well-being lies in decent work" (Annan, 2004). In order to reduce poverty in a sustainable manner and promote the development of a more just and equitable society, it is important to focus on expanding and improving opportunities for employment, with emphasis on both the quality and quantity of jobs.

An employment strategy aimed at promoting decent work under conditions of equality, security and dignity should be a fundamental component of any development strategy, and must be oriented to include employment creation in macroeconomic policy. Such a strategy also requires undertaking employment impact analysis as a basic criterion for macroeconomic policy and for policy decisions adopted in other areas. Furthermore, it calls for adopting specific measures to incorporate the informal sector in social protection programmes and for establishing incentive structures that promote employment creation by directing investment to sectors that are productive and labour-intensive, with a special view to promoting small and medium-sized enterprises.

In pursuing such a strategy, it is critical to invest in people, including their education, skill development, lifelong learning, and health and safety, and to improve market access for informal producers. The goal is to move workers and economic units into the mainstream so that they are covered by legal and institutional frameworks (International Labour Organization, 2002a). In addition, improvements in the policy and legal environment are needed to lower the costs of establishing and operating a business. Specific measures should include the development and application of simplified registration and licensing procedures, appropriate rules and regulations, and reasonable and fair taxation. Policies should be advanced to discourage businesses from shifting from the formal to the informal economy, and to enable new businesses to enter the formal economy and maintain labour standards. An expanded formal economy not only provides benefits for participants, but also helps to raise State revenues (International Labour Organization, 2002a).

Economic growth alone is not enough. Both productivity growth and employment creation are needed to reduce poverty in general and poverty among the working poor in particular. Regions of the world that have achieved both an increase in productivity levels over the long run and the creation of new employment opportunities for their growing labour forces have been the most successful in reducing overall poverty. As the ILO has observed, opportunities for decent employment address more than the income component of poverty; those who are able to secure decent jobs and receive adequate compensation, benefits and protection under the law are also empowered to voice their concerns and participate more actively in decision-making in the world of work, and are able to gain more respect for the work they do (International Labour Organization, 2005c).

Contrary to the expectations of development experts, the informal economy has not declined as a natural outgrowth of economic development but has instead expanded over the past two decades. Consequently, the policy prescriptions relating to the informal economy and inclusive development outlined at the World Summit for Social Development remain valid for achieving development and the reduction of inequality.

Informal enterprises should be integrated into the formal economy through access to affordable credit, exposure to information on markets and new technologies, and the ability to acquire technological and management skills. Further efforts should include extending labour standards and social protection to the informal economy without compromising its potential for generating employment (United Nations, 1995).

Governments should enhance their efforts in the area of youth employment. This is becoming increasingly important, as large and growing numbers of young people are entering the labour market and are unable to find work. The inability of the market to absorb them generates frustration and a sense of unfairness among youth and increases the likelihood of conflict.

Fostering social integration and cohesion

Consideration should be given to the importance of explicit policies to counter both the negative effects of globalization on social development and the new threats posed by market-driven reforms. Deliberate action must be taken to guarantee that cultural, religious and ethnic identities and rights are explicitly protected in international agreements and in national and local legislation, and that such protection translates into an enforceable code of conduct for national and transnational corporations and private interests operating under national jurisdictions. There is an urgent need to expand opportunities for participation in decision-making processes; in particular, specific areas of public policy formulation that have not yet incorporated participatory mechanisms should be identified, and steps should be taken to ensure unrestricted legal access to information among citizens in general and to establish mechanisms for the more open review of government policies.

Although targeting can be a useful approach to achieve equality, it should not become a substitute for universal coverage. From a social inclusion and empowerment standpoint, the economic benefits of targeting may be offset by the social costs. In addition to the feelings of stigmatization that targeting can generate, there is also the danger that non-targeted groups will grow resentful of those receiving assistance. In some cases, there may be little that separates a target group from a non-target group in terms of need. Under a targeted system, the determination of who receives assistance and who does not may be based on a variety of factors external to the level of need among individuals or groups, including donor preferences, programme design, political considerations or geographical location.

If targeting is to be employed, one of the more promising forms is community-based targeting, in which the community is directly involved in identifying beneficiaries using eligibility criteria of their own choosing. People at the community level are more likely than programme administrators to be aware of the actual circumstances in which people live, and the participatory process itself can be quite empowering for the community as it increases local control over programmes. Community-based targeting is an attractive option for two main reasons: it draws upon local knowledge, thereby increasing accuracy; and it involves beneficiaries directly in the decision-making process, thereby promoting equality (Devereux, 2002). Experience has shown that the most effective targeted programmes are those that are supported by specific institutions, involve community participation, and are backed up by adequate resources (Economic Commission for Latin America and the Caribbean, 2000b).

Notwithstanding the foregoing, evidence from different countries has shown that targeting can be counterproductive. Targeting programmes are often characterized by poor coverage and high cost, and can also provoke social divisions, discourage saving, jeopardize employment creation and encourage premature withdrawals from the labour force (Mesa-Lago, 2004). With a more universal approach to the provision of social services, many of the problems associated with targeting can be circumvented. The poor are mainstreamed along with other groups, thereby promoting social inclusion. Universal social services and benefits also carry the advantage of being more politically acceptable. When a broader range of people stand to benefit, it becomes easier to gain the support necessary to ensure the allocation of sufficient resources to put the universal protections in place. In developing countries, however, resource constraints pose the greatest challenge to pursuing this universal approach.

For indigenous peoples, poverty is closely linked with discrimination and the loss of control over their traditional lands and natural resources; therefore, programmes to alleviate poverty among these groups must be designed not only to facilitate social protection and social integration but also to address land and resource issues. With regard to this last aspect, the incorporation of indigenous history and culture in educational curricula can play an important role in reducing prejudices.

Since the creation of the United Nations, persons with disabilities have moved from accepting others' definitions of the parameters of their lives to becoming active in asserting strength and confidence in their own abilities to lead self-reliant and independent lives. The role of NGOs has been important in this process, and the efforts of the United Nations have contributed to the transformation as well. The consultations for the development of the Comprehensive and Integral Convention on the Protection and Promotion of the Rights and Dignity of Persons with Disabilities represent further proof of the prominence given to the issue of persons with disabilities. Programmes designed for persons with disabilities must emphasize equality of opportunities, both through individual rehabilitation and through the introduction of mechanisms for eliminating social and physical obstacles in order to facilitate their integration into society.

Governments should consider how their economic, social and environmental policies are likely to affect future generations and, by adhering to the implicit terms of the intergenerational contract, ensure that no generation lives at the expense of another. Steps should also be taken to identify and implement appropriate measures to address the societal impact of demographic shifts such as the growth of the ageing population in developed countries and the emergence of youth bulges in many developing countries.

The costs associated with old-age support are often covered by a combination of private resources and State-provided resources. In countries in which pensions are provided by the State, particularly in those relying on transfers from younger to older generations, the shortfall will be considerable over the coming decades owing to a significant decline in the relative proportion of contributors, and will eventually become unsustainable (World Bank, 1994; Chand and Jaeger, 1999; Bongaarts, 2004). To ensure that they are able to maintain pension systems compatible with the intergenerational contract, States should avoid depleting funds earmarked for pensions and old-age health coverage for future generations. A first step in this process would be to balance national budgets.

In recent years, the international agenda has been dominated by security issues and concerns relating to armed conflict. As one of the underlying causes of conflict is social disintegration, it is essential that Governments recognize that social integration is a key condition for creating and maintaining peaceful societies. Social integration can only be achieved by ensuring the full participation of all groups in the social, economic, political and cultural aspects of life. Two particular areas of concern are the challenges faced by youth, who are two to three times more likely than adults to be unemployed, and the horizontal inequalities between ethnic groups. It is essential that opportunities be provided for young people to obtain decent work and to participate in the political process; it is equally important to implement policies that counter horizontal inequalities. The most effective long-term solution is universal education. The enforcement of anti-discrimination legislation is crucial as well.

In conclusion, inclusive development incorporates the creation of an enabling environment that promotes more equitable access to income, resources and services, as well as international cooperation in the development of macroeconomic policies and in the liberalization of trade and investment in order to promote sustained economic growth and employment creation. The principles of equality should continue to guide social and economic policy-making to ensure that economic growth is conducive to social development, stability, fair competition and ethical conduct (United Nations, 1995). If this course of action is followed, inequality will no longer be the predicament it is today.

Notes

1 This chapter draws heavily from the "Review of the further implementation of the World Summit for Social Development and the outcome of the twenty-fourth special session of the General Assembly: report of the Secretary-General", submitted to the Commission for Social Development at its forty-third session (E/CN.5/2005/6; see United Nations, 2004c).

2 The people-centred approach to development was also highlighted at the 10-year review of the World Summit for Social Development (see E/CN.5/2005/L.2; United Nations, 2005a).

3 As noted in chapter III, the International Finance Facility would leverage new long-term donor commitments by issuing bonds in the capital markets, and special drawing rights could be particularly useful during times of crisis, as they would supplement the existing official reserves and could be used as an emergency financing facility to help countries overcome liquidity problems, to allow them to avoid borrowing at high market rates when attempting to build up their reserves, or to finance development (Atkinson, 2004).

Annex

The ten commitments of the World Summit for Social Development

At the World Summit for Social Development, held in March 1995, Governments adopted the Copenhagen Declaration on Social Development and Programme of Action of the World Summit for Social Development, and identified the eradication of poverty, the promotion of full employment and the fostering of social integration as goals of the highest priority for achieving secure, stable and just societies. At the heart of the Copenhagen Declaration are the ten commitments to social development agreed by the heads of State and Government at the Summit, which embody the global drive for social progress and development. The commitments are as follows:

Commitment 1: Create an enabling environment for social development

"We commit ourselves to creating an economic, political, social, cultural and legal environment that will enable people to achieve social development."

Commitment 2: Eradicate poverty

"We commit ourselves to the goal of eradicating poverty in the world, through decisive national actions and international cooperation, as an ethical, social, political and economic imperative of humankind."

Commitment 3: Support full employment

"We commit ourselves to promoting the goal of full employment as a basic priority of our economic and social policies, and to enabling all men and women to attain secure and sustainable livelihoods through freely chosen productive employment and work."

Commitment 4: Promote social integration

"We commit ourselves to promoting social integration by fostering societies that are stable, safe and just and that are based on the promotion and protection of all human rights, as well as on non-discrimination, tolerance, respect for diversity, equality of opportunity, solidarity, security, and participation of all people, including disadvantaged and vulnerable groups and persons."

Commitment 5: Achieve equality and equity between women and men

"We commit ourselves to promoting full respect for human dignity and to achieving equality and equity between women and men, and to recognizing and enhancing the participation and leadership roles of women in political, civil, economic, social and cultural life and in development."

Commitment 6: Attain universal and equitable access to quality education and primary health care

"We commit ourselves to promoting and attaining the goals of universal and equitable access to quality education, the highest attainable standard of physical and mental health, and the access of all to primary health care, making particular efforts to rectify inequalities relating to social conditions and without distinction as to race, national origin, gender, age or disability; respecting and promoting our common and particular cultures; striving to strengthen the role of culture in development; preserving the essential bases of people-centred sustainable development; and contributing to the full development of human resources and to social development. The purpose of these activities is to eradicate poverty, promote full and productive employment and foster social integration."

Commitment 7: Accelerate development in Africa and the least developed countries

"We commit ourselves to accelerating the economic, social and human resource development of Africa and the least developed countries."

Commitment 8: Ensure that structural adjustment programmes include social development goals

"We commit ourselves to ensuring that when structural adjustment programmes are agreed to they include social development goals, in particular eradicating poverty, promoting full and productive employment, and enhancing social integration."

Commitment 9: Increase significantly and/or utilize more efficiently the resources allocated to social development

"We commit ourselves to increasing significantly and/or utilizing more efficiently the resources allocated to social development in order to achieve the goals of the Summit through national action and regional and international cooperation."

Commitment 10: Promote an improved and strengthened framework for international, regional and subregional cooperation for social development

"We commit ourselves to an improved and strengthened framework for international, regional and subregional cooperation for social development, in a spirit of partnership, through the United Nations and other multilateral institutions."

Bibliography

Adams, R.H., Jr., and J. Page (2003). International migration, remittances and poverty in developing countries. World Bank Policy Research Working Paper, No. 3179. Washington, D.C.: World Bank. December.

Allen, J. (2003). Voices of migrants in Asia: a panorama of perspectives; voices, experiences and witness accounts of poor economic migrants in Asia. Paper presented at the Regional Conference on Migration, Development and Pro-Poor Policy Choices in Asia, Dhaka, 22-24 June.

Altimir, O. (1996). Economic development and social equity: a Latin American perspective. *Journal of Interamerican Studies and World Affairs* (summer/fall).

Annan, Kofi (2004). A fair globalization: implementing the Millennium Declaration. Address given on 20 September.

______ (2005a). Reducing risks from tsunamis: disaster and development. Policy brief. Available from http://www.undp.org/bcpr/disred/documents/tsunami/undp/rdrtsunamis.pdf (accessed 18 April 2005).

______ (2005b). Remarks at a Security Council meeting on cross-border problems in West Africa, New York, 25 February.

Atkinson, A.B. (2003). Income inequality in OECD countries: notes and explanations. Mimeo. Oxford.

______, ed. (2004). *New Sources of Development Finance*. United Nations University/World Institute for Development Economics Research (UNU/WIDER) Studies in Development Economics. New York: Oxford University Press.

Bales, K. (2000). *Disposable People: New Slavery in the Global Economy*. Los Angeles: University of California Press.

Barro, R. (1991). Economic growth in a cross section of countries. *Quarterly Journal of Economics,* vol. 106, No. 2, pp. 407-443.

______, and X. Sala-i-Martin (1992). Convergence. *Journal of Political Economy* (April), p. 100.

Behrman, J., N. Birdsall and M. Szekely (2000). Economic reform and wage differentials in Latin America. IADB Research Working Paper, No. 435. Washington, D.C.: Inter-American Development Bank.

Ben-David, D. (1993). Equalizing exchange: trade liberalization and income convergence. *Quarterly Journal of Economics*, vol. 108, No. 3, pp. 653-679.

Berry, A., and J. Serieux (2002). Riding the elephants: the evolution of world economic growth and income distribution at the end of the 20th century (1980-2000). Unpublished manuscript. Toronto: Centre for International Studies, University of Toronto.

______ (2004). All about the giants: probing the influences on world growth and income inequality at the end of the 20th century. Center for Economic Studies and Ifo Institute for Economic Research. *CESifo Economic Studies*, vol. 50, No. 1/2004, pp. 139-175.

Bigsten, A. (2000). Globalisation and income inequality in Uganda. Paper presented at the Conference on Poverty and Inequality in Developing Countries: A Policy Dialogue on the Effects of Globalisation, Paris, 30 November – 1 December 2000. Paris: Organisation for Economic Cooperation and Development.

Birdsall, N. (2002). A stormy day on an open field: asymmetry and convergence in the global economy. Paper presented at the 2002 Reserve Bank of Australia Conference on Globalization, Living Standards and Inequality: Recent Progress and Continuing Challenges, Sydney, 26-28 May. Available from http://www.rba.gov.au/PublicationsAndResearch/Conferences/2002/Birdsall.pdf (accessed 31 January 2005).

______, D. Ross and R.H. Sabot (1995). Inequality and growth reconsidered: lessons from East Asia. *World Bank Economic Review*, vol. 9, No. 3 (September), pp. 477-508.

Bongaarts, J. (2004). Population aging and the rising cost of public pensions. *Population and Development Review*, vol. 30, No. 1, pp. 1-23.

Bourguignon, F. (1999). Crime, violence and inequitable development. Paper prepared for the Annual World Bank Conference on Development Economics, Washington, D.C., 28-30 June.

______, and C. Morrison (2002). Inequality among world citizens: 1820-1992. *American Economic Review*, vol. 92, No. 4 (September).

Brody, Jennifer (2002). The global epidemic of childhood obesity: poverty, urbanization, and the nutrition transition. *Nutrition Bytes*, vol. 8, No. 2, article 1.

Caprio, G., and D. Klingebiel (1996). Bank insolvencies: cross country experience. World Bank Policy Research Working Paper, No. 1620. Washington, D.C.: World Bank.

Cardoso, F.H. (1995). Estado, mercado, democracia: ¿Existe una perspectiva Latinoamericana? *Socialismo y Participación* (Lima), vol. 71 (September), pp. 85-94.

______ (2004). Civil society and global governance. Paper presented to the Panel of Eminent Persons on United Nations – Civil Society Relations, New York, 2-3 June, p. 3.

Carr, Marilyn, and Martha Alter Chen (2002). Globalization and the informal economy: how global trade and investment impact on the working poor. Working Paper on the Informal Economy, Employment Sector, No. 2002/1. Geneva: International Labour Office, pp. 2, 6, 7 and 9.

Castro-Leal, F., and others (1999). Public social spending in Africa: Do the poor benefit? *World Bank Research Observer*, vol. 14, No. 1, pp. 49-72.

Chand, S.K., and A. Jaeger (1999). Aging Populations and Public Pension Schemes. Occasional Paper, No. 147. Washington, D.C.: International Monetary Fund.

Charmes, Jacques (1998). Informal sector, poverty, and gender: a review of empirical evidence. Background paper commissioned for the *World Development Report, 2000/2001*. Washington, D.C.: World Bank.

Chen, Martha, Renana Jhabvala and Frances Lund (2002). Supporting workers in the informal economy: a policy framework. ILO Working Paper on the Informal Economy, Employment Sector, No. 2002/2. Geneva: International Labour Office, pp. 2, 3, 11, 13, 25 and 39.

______, Jennifer Sebstad and Leslie O'Connell (1999). Counting the invisible workforce: the case of homebased workers. *World Development*, vol. 27, No. 3, pp. 603-610.

Chen, Shohua, and M. Ravallion (2000). How did the world's poorest fare in the 1990s? World Bank Policy Research Working Series, Paper No. WPS 2409. Washington, D.C.: World Bank Development Research Group.

Chopra, M., S. Galbraith and I. Darnton-Hill (2002). A global response to a global problem: the epidemic of overnutrition. *Bulletin of the World Health Organization,* vol. 80, No. 12. Geneva: World Health Organization.

Chu, K., H. Davoodi and S. Gupta (2000). Income distribution and tax and government social spending policies in developing countries. United Nations University/World Institute for Development Economics Research (UNU/WIDER) Working Paper, No. 214. Helsinki.

Cichon, M. (1997). Are there better ways to cut and share the cake? The European welfare states at the crossroads. Issues in Social Protection Discussion, Paper No. 3. Geneva: International Labour Office.

Commission for Africa (2005). *Our Common Interest: Report of the Commission for Africa*. March. Available from http://www.commissionforafrica.org/english/report/thereport/english/11-03-05_cr_report.pdf (accessed 20 April 2005).

Commission on Human Security (2003). *Human Security Now: Protecting and Empowering People*. United Nations publication, Sales No. 03.III.U.2; published with Communications Development Inc., Washington, D.C., p. 17.

Copeland, Brian R., and M. Scott Taylor (2004). Trade liberalization and poverty: the evidence so far. *The Journal of Economic Literature*, vol. XLII, No. 1 (March), pp. 72-115.

Cornia, G.A. (2004). Inequality, growth and poverty: an overview of changes over the last two decades. In *Inequality, Growth, and Poverty in an Era of Liberalization and Globalization*, G.A. Cornia, ed. Oxford: Oxford University Press, p. 11.

______, T. Addison and S. Kiiski (2004). Income distribution changes and their impact in the post-World War II period. In *Inequality, Growth and Poverty in an Era of Liberalization and Globalization*, G.A. Cornia, ed. Oxford: Oxford University Press.

______, and J. Court (2001). *Inequality, Growth and Poverty in the Era of Liberalization and Globalization.* United Nations University/World Institute for Development Economics Research (UNU/WIDER) Policy Brief, No. 4. Helsinki.

______, and S. Kiiski (2001). *Trends in Income Distribution in the Post-World War II Period: Evidence and Interpretation.* United Nations University/World Institute for Development Economics Research (UNU/WIDER) Discussion Paper, No. 89. Helsinki.

______, and Leonardo Menchini (2005). The pace and distribution of health improvements during the last 40 years: some preliminary results. Draft paper prepared for the UNDP-French Government Sponsored Forum on Human Development, Paris, 17-19 January 2005.

Dealogic (2004). Analytics and Market Data/ProjectWare. Available from http://www.dealogic.com (accessed 4 June 2004).

Deininger, K., and L. Squire (1998). New ways of looking at old issues: inequality and growth. *Journal of Development Economics*, vol. 57, No. 2 (December), pp. 259-287.

Dessalegn, R. (1987) *Famine and Survival Strategies: A Case Study from Northeast Ethiopia.* Food and Famine Monograph Series, No. 1. Addis Ababa University, Institute of Development Studies.

Devereux, Stephen (2002). *Social Protection for the Poor: Lessons from Recent International Experience.* Institute of Development Studies, Working Paper No. 142. Brighton, Sussex, United Kingdom. January, p. 11.

Diwan, I. (1999). Labour shares and financial crises. Preliminary draft. Washington, D.C.: World Bank.

Dreze, J., and A. Sen (1989). *Hunger and Public Action.* Oxford: Clarendon Press.

Dwan, Renata, and Micaela Gustavsson (2004). Major armed conflicts. *SIPRI Yearbook, 2004: Armaments, Disarmament and International Security.* Oxford: Oxford University Press.

Easterly, W. (2001). The effect of IMF and World Bank programs on poverty. Paper prepared for the United Nations University/World Institute for Development Economics Research (UNU/WIDER) Development Conference on Growth and Poverty, Helsinki, 25-26 May.

Economic Commission for Africa (2003). *Economic Report on Africa, 2003: Accelerating the Pace of Development.* United Nations publication, Sales No. E.03.II.K.1. Addis Ababa.

Economic Commission for Latin America and the Caribbean (1997). *The Equity Gap: Latin America, the Caribbean and the Social Summit.* United Nations publication, Sales No. E.97.II.G.11. Santiago de Chile.

______ (2000a). *Equity, Development and Citizenship.* United Nations publication, Sales No. E.01.II.G.89. Santiago de Chile.

______ (2000b). The equity gap: a second assessment. Paper prepared for the Second Regional Conference in Follow-up to the World Summit for Social Development, Santiago de Chile, May.

______ (2005a). *Economic Survey of Latin America and the Caribbean, 1999-2000*. United Nations publication, Sales No. E.00.II.G.2. Available from http://www.cepal.org/publicaciones/DesarrolloEconomico/2/LCG2102PI/lcg2102iChapterVI.pdf (accessed 18 April 2005).

______ (2005b). Latin America and the Caribbean 10 years after the Social Summit: a regional overview. Paper submitted to the Panel Discussion of Regional Commissions on the Follow-up to Copenhagen during the forty-third session of the Commission for Social Development, New York, 9-18 February.

The Economist (2004). In the shadows. 17 June, p. 92.

Equator Principles (2004). The Equator Principles: an industry approach for financial institutions in determining, assessing and managing environmental & social risk in project financing. Available from http://www.equator-principles.com/documents/Equator_Principles.pdf (accessed 18 April 2005).

Fajnzylber, P., D. Lederman and N. Loayza (2002). Inequality and violent crime. *Journal of Law and Economics*, vol. 45, No. 1, pp. 1-40. Washington, D.C.: World Bank.

Farrell, Diana (2004). The hidden dangers of the informal economy. *McKinsey Quarterly*, No. 3.

Feige, Edgar L. (1989). *The Underground Economies: Tax Evasion and Information Distortion*. Cambridge, New York and Melbourne: Cambridge University Press.

______ (1994). The underground economy and the currency enigma. In *Public Finance and Irregular Activity*, Werner W. Pommerehne, ed. *Supplement to Public Finance/Finances Publique*, vol. 49, No. 46, pp. 119-136.

Fischer, R. (2000). The evolution of inequality after trade liberalization. Discussion draft. Universidad de Chile.

Flegal, K.M., and others (1998). Overweight and obesity in the United States: prevalence and trends, 1960-1994. *International Journal of Obesity and Related Metabolic Disorders*, vol. 22, No. 1, pp. 39-47.

Food and Agriculture Organization of the United Nations (2000). *Global Network on Integrated Soil Management for Sustainable Use of Salt-Affected Soils*. Land and Plant Nutrition Management Service. Available from http://www.fao.org/ag/AGL/agll/spush/intro.htm. (accessed 7 April 2005).

______ (2002). The developing world's new burden: obesity. Available from http://www.fao.org/FOCUS/E/obesity/obes1.htm (accessed 7 April 2005).

______ (2004). *The State of Food Insecurity in the World, 2004: Monitoring Progress towards the World Food Summit and Millennium Development Goals*. Rome.

______ (2005a). *The State of Food Insecurity in the World, 2004*. United Nations publication, Sales No. E.05.LI.4.

______(2005b). *State of the World's Forests, 2005*. United Nations publication, Sales No. E.05.II.E.10.

Frey, Bruno S., and Werner Pommerehne (1984). The hidden economy: State and prospects for measurement. *Review of Income and Wealth*, vol. 30, No. 1, pp. 1-23.

Galbraith, J.K., and L. Jiaqing (1999). Inequality and financial crises: some early findings. University of Texas Inequality Project Working Paper, No. 9. Austin: University of Texas at Austin/LBJ School of Public Affairs.

García, A.B., and J.V. Gruat (2003). Social protection: a life cycle continuum investment for social justice, poverty reduction and sustainable development (version 1.0). Geneva: International Labour Office.

Geda, A. (2004). Openness, inequality and poverty in Africa: exploring the role of global interdependence. Paper prepared for the workshop on regional studies, held on 17 and 18 June in preparation for the fourth meeting of the International Forum for Social Development: Equity, Inequalities and Interdependence, held in New York on 5 and 6 October.

Global Fund to Fight AIDS, Tuberculosis and Malaria (2005). Available from http://www.theglobalfund.org/en/in_action/events/worldtbday/2005/ (accessed 19 April 2005).

de Graaf, Paul M., and M. Kalmijn (2001). Trends in the intergenerational transmission of cultural and economic status. *Acta Sociologica*, vol. 44, pp. 51-66.

Grumberg, I., and S. Khan (2000). *Globalization: The United Nations Development Dialogue; Finance, Trade, Poverty, Peace-Building*. New York: United Nations University Press.

Guadagni, Alieto Aldo (2004). Comercio, desarrollo y pobreza. Available from http://www.eclac.cl/prensa/noticias/comunicados/1/14671/GuadagnipresentacionCEPAL040504.pdf, pp. 22-25.

Guimarães, Roberto (1996). ¿El leviatán en extinción? Notas sobre la reforma del Estado en América Latina. *Pretextos* (Lima), No. 9 (November), pp. 115-143.

______ (2004) Waiting for Godot: sustainable development, international trade and governance in environmental policies. *Contemporary Politics*, vol. 10, Nos. 3-4 (September-December).

Gurr, Ted Robert (1968). Psychological factors in civil violence. *World Politics*, vol. 20, No. 2, pp. 245-278.

Gustaffson, B., and M. Johansson (1999). In search of smoking guns: What makes income inequality vary over time in different countries? *American Sociological Review*, vol. 64, pp. 586-605.

Harrison, B., and B. Bluestone (1988). *The Great U-Turn*. New York: Basic Books.

HelpAge International (2004). *Age and Security: How Social Pensions Can Deliver Effective Aid to Poor Older People and Their Families.* London: HelpAge International.

Heyzer, Noeleen (2002). Combating trafficking in women and children: a gender and human rights framework. Plenary address at the Conference on the Human Rights Challenge of Globalization: Asia-Pacific-US: The Trafficking in Persons, Especially Women and Children. Honolulu, 13-15 November.

Human Rights Watch (2004). *Human Rights Watch World Report, 2004: Human Rights and Armed Conflict.* New York: Human Rights Watch.

Humphreys, Macartan (2003). *Economics and violent conflict.* Cambridge, Massachusetts: Harvard University.

Iadicola, Peter, and Anson Shupe (2003). *Violence, Inequality, and Human Freedom,* 2nd edition. New York: Rowman & Littlefield Publishers, pp. 154-155.

Instituto de Promoción de la Economía Social (1999). *IPES 1998/1999: Facing Up to Inequality in Latin America.* Washington, D.C.: Inter-American Development Bank.

International Fund for Agricultural Development (2004). Over one billion people lack access to basic financial services. IFAD Press Release, No. 38/04. November.

International Labour Conference (2005). *A Global Alliance against Forced Labour: Global Report under the Follow-up to the ILO Declaration on Fundamental Principles and Rights at Work 2005.* Report I (B), submitted to the International Labour Conference at its 93rd session, Geneva, 31 May – 16 June. Geneva: International Labour Office.

International Labour Organization (1997). *World Labour Report, 1997-98: Industrial Relations, Democracy and Social Stability.* Geneva: International Labour Office, pp. 237-238.

______ (2002a). Conclusions concerning decent work and the informal economy. Adopted by the International Labour Conference at its 90th session, Geneva, 3-20 June. *International Labour Conference Provisional Record* (Geneva), No. 25, para. 9.

______ (2002b). *Women and Men in the Informal Economy: A Statistical Picture.* Geneva: International Labour Office/Employment Sector.

______ (2003). Working out of Poverty: Report of the Director-General. Paper submitted to the International Labour Conference at its 91st session, Geneva, 3-19 June. Geneva: International Labour Office, p. 73.

______ (2004). *Report of the World Commission on the Social Dimension of Globalization—A Fair Globalization: Creating Opportunities for All.* Geneva: International Labour Office, paras. 262-264.

______ (2005a). Database on Key Indicators of the Labour Market (KILM). Available from http://www.ilo.org/public/english/employment/strat/kilm/kilm08.htm (accessed 25 February 2005).

______ (2005b). Decent work—the heart of social progress. Available from http://www.ilo.org/public/english/decent.htm (accessed 2 May 2005).

______ (2005c). *World Employment Report 2004-05: Employment, Productivity and Poverty Reduction*. Geneva: International Labour Office, p. 24.

International Monetary Fund and International Development Association (2003). *Heavily Indebted Poor Countries (HIPC) Initiative—Status of Implementation*. Washington, D.C.

Jackson, Tim, and Laurie Michaelis (2003). *Policies for Sustainable Consumption: A Report to the Sustainable Development Commission*. London.

Jelin, Elizabeth, and Rita Díaz-Muñoz (2003). Major trends affecting families: South America in perspective. In *Major Trends Affecting Families: A Background Document*. New York: United Nations, Department of Economic and Social Affairs, p. 119.

Johnson, Simon, Daniel Kaufmann and Andrei Schleifler (1997). The unofficial economy in transition. *Brookings Papers on Economic Activity*, No. 2. Washington D.C.: The Brookings Institution, pp. 159-239.

Joint United Nations Programme on HIVAIDS (2004). *AIDS Epidemic Update, December 2004*. Available from http://www.unaids.org/wad2004/report.html (accessed 13 April 2005).

Jomo, K.S. (2003). Globalization, liberalization and equitable development: lessons from East Asia. Overarching Concerns Paper, No. 3. Geneva: United Nations Research Institute for Social Development. July.

______ (2004). Growth with equity in East Asia? Paper prepared for the workshop on regional studies, held on 17 and 18 June in preparation for the fourth meeting of the International Forum for Social Development: Equity, Inequalities and Interdependence, held in New York on 5 and 6 October.

Kelly, P., and V. Saiz-Omeñaca (2004). The allocation of government expenditures in the world, 1990-2001. Unpublished paper. November.

Klare, Michael T. (1995). The global trade in light weapons and the international system in the post-cold war era. In *Lethal Commerce*, Jeffrey Boutwell, Michael T. Klare and Laura W. Reed, eds. Cambridge, Massachusetts: American Academy of Arts and Sciences, Committee on International Security Studies.

Kramer, R. (2000). Poverty, inequality and youth violence. *The Annals of the American Academy of Political Science*, vol. 567, No. 1 (January).

Lindert, P., and J .Williamson (2001). Does globalization make the world more equal? NBER Working Paper, No. 8228. Paper presented at the National Bureau of Economic Research Conference on Globalization in Historical Perspective, Santa Barbara, California, 3-6 May.

Lloyd-Sherlock, P. (2000). Old age and poverty in developing countries: new policy challenges. *World Development*, vol. 28, No. 12, pp. 2157-2168.

Lowi, T. (2001). Our millennium: political science confronts the global corporate economy. *International Political Science Review*, vol. 22, No. 2, pp. 131-150.

Mayer-Foulkes, D. (2001). Convergence clubs in cross-country life expectancy dynamics. United Nations University/World Institute for Development Economics Research (UNU/WIDER) Discussion Paper, No. 2001/134. Helsinki.

Melchior, A., K. Telle and H. Wiig (2000). Globalization and inequality. Studies on Foreign Policy Issues, Report 6B. Oslo: Royal Norwegian Ministry of Foreign Affairs.

Mesa-Lago, Carmelo (2004). Models of development, social policy and reform and Latin America. In *Social Policy in a Development Context*, Thandika Mkandawire, ed. Geneva: United Nations Research Institute for Social Development, pp. 175-204.

Milanovic, B. (1998). *Income, Inequality and Poverty during the Transition from Planned to Market Economy*. Washington, D.C.: World Bank.

Morales-Gomez, D. (1999). A new development paradigm. Ottawa: International Development Research Centre. Available from http://web.idrc.ca/en/ev-27516-201-1-DO_TOPIC.html (accessed 17 May 2005).

Morley, S. (2000). Distribution and growth in Latin America in an era of structural reform. Paper presented at the Conference on Poverty and Inequality in Developing Countries: A Policy Dialogue on the Effects of Globalization. Paris, OECD Development Centre, 30 November – 1 December.

Narayan, Deepa, and others, eds. (2000). *Voices of the Poor: Crying Out for Change*. Oxford and New York: Oxford University Press (for the World Bank).

Norwegian Agency for Development Cooperation (2003). *Review of Nordic Monitoring of the World Bank and IMF Support to the PRSP Process*. Oslo, p. 23.

Ocampo, José Antonio (2002a). Developing countries' anti-cyclical policies in a globalized world. In *Development Economics and Structuralist Macroeconomics: Essays in Honour of Lance Taylor*, Amitava Dutt and Jaime Ros, eds. Cheltenham: Edward Elgar.

______ (2002b). Rethinking the development agenda. *Cambridge Journal of Economics*, vol. 26, No. 3, pp. 393-407.

______ (2005). Globalization, development and democracy. Paper prepared for the first annual International Forum for Development, New York, 18-19 October 2004. Also in *Items and Issues*, vol. 5, No. 3, pp. 11-20.

______, and Juan Martin (2003). *Globalization and Development: A Latin American and Caribbean Perspective*. Palo Alto, California: Stanford University Press; and Santiago de Chile, Economic Commission for Latin America and the Caribbean.

ORC Macro (2005). MEASURE DHS STATcompiler. Available from http://www.measuredhs.com (accessed 15 February 2005).

Organisation for Economic Cooperation and Development (2001). *The DAC Guidelines: Helping Prevent Violent Conflict.* Paris.

________ (2003). Final ODA data for 2003. Available from http://www.oecd.org/dataoecd/19/52/34352584.pdf (accessed 12 May 2005).

_______ (2005a). Development Assistance Committee (DAC) International Development Statistics (IDS) online. Available from www.oecd.org/dac/stats/idsonline.

________(2005b). Official Development Assistance increases further—but 2006 targets still a challenge. 11 April 2005. Available from http://www.oecd.org/document/3/0,2340,en_2649_201185_34700611_1_1_1_1,00.html (accessed 20 April 2005).

Petersilia, Joan (2001). Invisible victims: violence against persons with developmental disabilities. *Criminal Justice and Behaviour,* vol. 28, No. 6 (December), pp. 655-694.

Pinstrup-Andersen, P., and J. Babinard (2001). Globalization and human nutrition: opportunities and risks for the poor in developing countries, *African Journal of Food and Nutritional Sciences,* vol. 1, pp. 9-18.

Ravallion, M. (2004). Growth, inequality and poverty: looking beyond averages. In *Growth, Inequality and Poverty: Prospects for Pro-Poor Economic Development,* Anthony Shorrocks and Rolph van der Hoeven, eds. United Nations University/World Institute for Development Economics Research (UNU/WIDER) Studies in Development Economics. Oxford: Oxford University Press. Chap. 3, table 3.1, p. 69.

Rawls, J. (1971). *A Theory of Justice.* Cambridge, Massachusetts: Belknap Press/Harvard University Press.

Razavi, S. (2005). Women, work and social policy. *UNRISD News* (Geneva), No. 27 (March), p. 6-7.

Renner, Michael (1999). *Ending Violent Conflict.* Worldwatch Paper, No. 146 (April). Washington, D.C.: Worldwatch Institute, p. 40.

Ricupero, Rubens (2001). A face visível da desigualdade. *A Folha de São Paulo* (8 July). Available from http://www.jornal.ufrj.br/newsletter/ anteriores/news138.html#28_ (accessed 20 April 2005).

Rodrik, D (2002). Globalization for whom? Time to change the rules—and focus on poor workers. *Harvard Magazine,* vol. 104, No. 6 (July-August), p. 29.

Roper, J., and R.W. Roberts (1999). Deforestation: tropical forests in decay. Forestry Advisors Network of the Canadian International Development Agency (CFAN-CIDA). Available from http://www.rcfa-cfan.org/index.html (accessed 9 February 2005).

Sahn, David E., David Stifel and Stephen Younger (1999). Inter-temporal changes in welfare: preliminary results from nine African countries. Cornell Food and Nutrition Policy Program Working Paper, No. 94. Ithaca, New York: Cornell University.

______, and Stephen Younger (2000). Expenditure incidence in Africa: microeconomic evidence. *Fiscal Studies*, vol. 21, No. 3, pp. 329-347.

Sainz, P. (2004). Poverty, unemployment and income distribution evolution in the nineties. Paper prepared for the workshop on regional studies, held on 17 and 18 June in preparation for the fourth meeting of the International Forum for Social Development: Equity, Inequalities and Interdependence, held in New York on 5 and 6 October.

Sala-i-Martin, Xavier (2002). The disturbing "rise" of global income inequality. NBER Working Paper, No. 8902. Cambridge, Massachusetts: National Bureau of Economic Research. April.

Sanne, Christer (1997). Lifestyle and consumption: prospects of cutting consumption in wealthy countries. Paper presented at the Conference on Environmental Justice: Global Ethics for the 21st Century, Melbourne, Australia, 1-3 October, pp. 1-8.

Schneider, Friedrich (2002). Size and measurement of the informal economy in 110 countries around the world. World Bank Working Paper. July.

Schölvinck, Johan (1996). Environment and quality of life in urban areas: production, consumption and environmental degradation. In *Proceedings and Recommendations of the International Symposium on Human Settlements and Habitat, 31 March – 2 April 1996*, Dolores A. Wozniak and others, eds. San Diego: International Institute for Human Resources Development, pp. 2-8.

Sen, Amartya (1995). *Inequality Re-examined.* Cambridge, Massachusetts: Harvard University Press.

______ (1999). *Development as Freedom.* New York: Anchor Books/Random House, Inc.

Shaw, M., J. van Dijk and W. Rhomberg (2003). Determining trends in global crime and justice: an overview of results. *Forum on Crime and Society*, vol. 3, Nos. 1-2.

Skeldon, R. (2002). Migration and poverty. *Asia-Pacific Population Journal*, vol. 17, No. 4 (December). Bangkok: Economic and Social Commission for Asia and the Pacific.

SOPEMI (Continuous Reporting System on Migration) (2003). *Trends in International Migration: Annual Report, 2002 Edition.* Paris: Organisation for Economic Cooperation and Development.

South-North Development Monitor (2005). Argentina: economic growth doing little to reduce rich-poor gap. No. 5773 (5 April). Available from http://www.sunsonline.org/contents.php?num=5773 (accessed 20 April 2005).

Spilimbergo, A.J., L. Londoño and M. Skézely (1999). Income distribution, factor endowments and trade openness. *Journal of Development Economics*, vol. 59, pp. 77-101.

Stiglitz, J. (1998). More instruments and broader goals: moving toward the post-Washington consensus. Paper presented at the United Nations University/

World Institute for Development Economics Research (UNU/WIDER) Annual Lecture, Helsinki, 7 January. UNU/WIDER Working Paper, No. 215.

Stockholm International Peace Research Institute (2003). SIPRI *Yearbook, 2003: Armaments, Disarmament and International Security*. Oxford: Oxford University Press.

______ (2004). *SIPRI Yearbook, 2004: Armaments, Disarmament and International Security*. Oxford: Oxford University Press.

Taylor, L. (2004) External liberalization, economic performance, and distribution in Latin America and elsewhere. In *Inequality, Growth, and Poverty in an Era of Liberalization and Globalization*, G.A. Cornia, ed. Oxford: Oxford University Press.

Timmer P.C., and A.S. Timmer (2004). Reflections on launching three books about poverty, inequality, and economic growth. *WIDER Angle*, No. 1, p. 3.

Trebilcock, Anne (2004). Decent work and the informal economy. Paper submitted to the Conference on Unlocking Human Potential: Linking the Informal and Formal Sectors, Helsinki, 17-18 September, organized by the Expert Group on Development Issues (EGDI) and United Nations University/ World Institute for Development Economics Research (UNU/WIDER), p. 20.

United Nations (1995). *Report of the World Summit for Social Development, Copenhagen, 6-12 March 1995*. Sales No. E.96.IV.8.

______ (1996). Changing consumption and production patterns: report of the Secretary-General. E/CN.17/1996/5. 30 January. Submitted to the Commission on Sustainable Development at its fourth session, New York, 18 April – 3 May.

______ (2000). United Nations Millennium Declaration. General Assembly resolution 55/2. 18 December.

______ (2001). Prevention of armed conflict: report of the Secretary-General. A/55/985-S/2001/574. 7 June.

______ (2003a). Improving public sector effectiveness: report of the Secretary-General. E/CN.5/2004/5. 3 December. Submitted to the Commission for Social Development at its forty-second session, New York, 4-13 February 2004.

______ (2003b). *Report on the World Social Situation—Social Vulnerability: Sources and Challenges*. Sales No. E/03/IV/10.

________(2003c). *World Population Prospects: The 2002 Revision*. Department of Economic and Social Affairs, Population Division.

______ (2004a). *Human Rights and Poverty Reduction: A Conceptual Framework*. New York and Geneva: Office of the High Commissioner for Human Rights

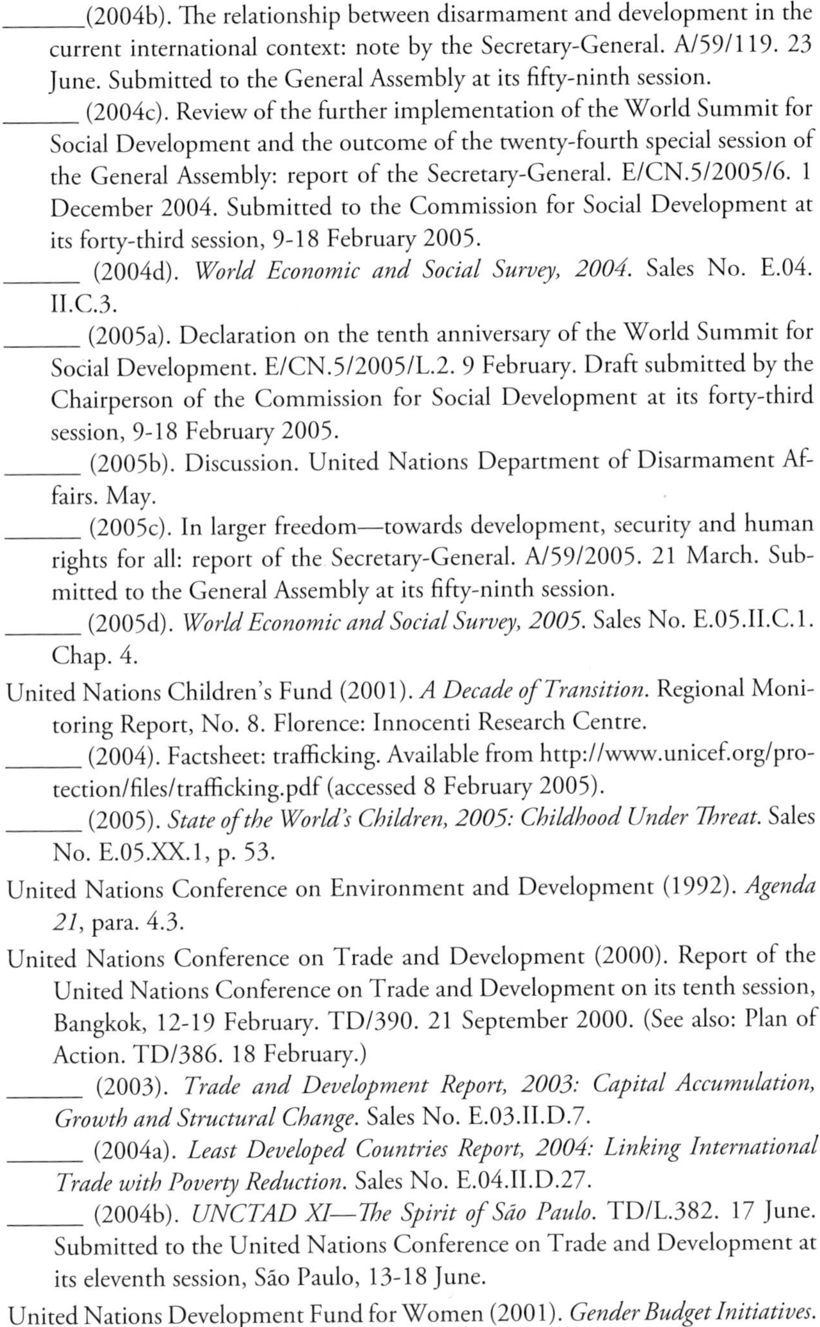

______(2004b). The relationship between disarmament and development in the current international context: note by the Secretary-General. A/59/119. 23 June. Submitted to the General Assembly at its fifty-ninth session.

______ (2004c). Review of the further implementation of the World Summit for Social Development and the outcome of the twenty-fourth special session of the General Assembly: report of the Secretary-General. E/CN.5/2005/6. 1 December 2004. Submitted to the Commission for Social Development at its forty-third session, 9-18 February 2005.

______ (2004d). *World Economic and Social Survey, 2004*. Sales No. E.04. II.C.3.

______ (2005a). Declaration on the tenth anniversary of the World Summit for Social Development. E/CN.5/2005/L.2. 9 February. Draft submitted by the Chairperson of the Commission for Social Development at its forty-third session, 9-18 February 2005.

______ (2005b). Discussion. United Nations Department of Disarmament Affairs. May.

______ (2005c). In larger freedom—towards development, security and human rights for all: report of the Secretary-General. A/59/2005. 21 March. Submitted to the General Assembly at its fifty-ninth session.

______ (2005d). *World Economic and Social Survey, 2005*. Sales No. E.05.II.C.1. Chap. 4.

United Nations Children's Fund (2001). *A Decade of Transition*. Regional Monitoring Report, No. 8. Florence: Innocenti Research Centre.

______ (2004). Factsheet: trafficking. Available from http://www.unicef.org/protection/files/trafficking.pdf (accessed 8 February 2005).

______ (2005). *State of the World's Children, 2005: Childhood Under Threat*. Sales No. E.05.XX.1, p. 53.

United Nations Conference on Environment and Development (1992). *Agenda 21*, para. 4.3.

United Nations Conference on Trade and Development (2000). Report of the United Nations Conference on Trade and Development on its tenth session, Bangkok, 12-19 February. TD/390. 21 September 2000. (See also: Plan of Action. TD/386. 18 February.)

______ (2003). *Trade and Development Report, 2003: Capital Accumulation, Growth and Structural Change*. Sales No. E.03.II.D.7.

______ (2004a). *Least Developed Countries Report, 2004: Linking International Trade with Poverty Reduction*. Sales No. E.04.II.D.27.

______ (2004b). *UNCTAD XI—The Spirit of São Paulo*. TD/L.382. 17 June. Submitted to the United Nations Conference on Trade and Development at its eleventh session, São Paulo, 13-18 June.

United Nations Development Fund for Women (2001). *Gender Budget Initiatives*. New York. Published with the Commonwealth Secretariat, London; and International Development Research Centre, Ottawa, p. 1. Available from http://www.gender-budgets.org/uploads/user-S/10999516661ACF31B2.pdf (accessed 2 March 2005).

______ (2003). *Not a Minute More: Ending Violence Against Women*, p. 17.

United Nations Development Programme (1998). *Human Development Report, 1998: Changing Today's Consumption Patterns—for Tomorrow's Human Development*. Sales No. 98.III.B.41. New York: Oxford University Press. Overview, p. 2.

______ (1999). *Human Development Report, 1999: Globalization with a Human Face*. Sales No. E.99.III.B.40. New York: Oxford University Press.

______ (2002). *Human Development Report, 2002: Deepening Democracy in a Fragmented World*. Sales No. E.02.III.B.1. New York: Oxford University Press. Chap. 1.

______ (2003). *Human Development Report, 2003—Millennium Development Goals: A Compact among Nations to End Human Poverty*. Sales No. E.03.III.B.1. New York: Oxford University Press.

______ (2004a). Draft country programme document for the Republic of Azerbaijan (2005-2009). Paper presented at the 2004 annual session of the Executive Board, Geneva, 14-23 June.

______ (2004b). *Human Development Report, 2004: Cultural Liberty in Today's Diverse World*. Sales No. E.04.III.B.1. New York: Oxford University Press.

United Nations Educational, Scientific and Cultural Organization (2005). *Education For All, 2005: The Quality Imperative*. Global Monitoring Report. Paris.

United Nations Environment Programme (2002). *The Sustainability of Development in Latin America and the Caribbean*. Sales No. E.02.II.G.48. Published with the Economic Commission for Latin America and the Caribbean, Santiago de Chile, pp. 147-148.

United Nations High Commissioner for Refugees (2005a). Asylum levels and trends in industrialized countries, 2004: overview of asylum applications lodged in Europe and non-European industrialized countries in 2004. March.

______ (2005b). *Refugees: 2004 Year in Review*, vol. 4, No. 137 (January).

United Nations Millennium Project (2005). *Investing in Development: A Practical Plan to Achieve the Millennium Development Goals*. New York, p. 263.

United Nations Population Fund (2005). Trafficking in human misery. Available from http://www.unfpa.org/gender/trafficking.htm (accessed 5 February 2005).

United Nations Research Institute for Social Development (2005). Executive summary. *Gender Equality: Striving for Justice in an Unequal World*. Paris, p. 13.

United States Department of Justice (2004). *Bureau of Justice Statistics: Crime Data Brief*. Washington, D.C.: Office of Justice Programs. November.

United States Department of State (2004). *Trafficking in Persons Report: June 2004*. Washington, D.C.

United States General Accounting Office (2000). Public health: trends in tuberculosis in the United States. *Report to Congressional Requesters*, No. GAO-01-82. Washington, D.C. October.

Urdal, Henrik (2004). The devil in the demographics: the effect of youth bulges on domestic armed conflict, 1950-2000. Social Development Papers: Conflict and Reconstruction Paper, No. 14. Oslo: International Peace Research Institute. July.

Walker, A. (1993). My mother and father's keeper? The social and economic features of intergenerational solidarity. Paper presented at the Conference on the Finnish Welfare State at the Edge of Change. Jyvaskyla, Finland, 26 May. Helsinki: National Research and Development Centre for Welfare and Health.

Weeks, J. (2004). Trends in inequality in the developed OECD countries: changing the agenda. Paper prepared for the workshop on regional studies, held on 17 and 18 June in preparation for the fourth meeting of the International Forum for Social Development: Equity, Inequalities and Interdependence, held in New York on 5 and 6 October.

Women in Informal Employment: Globalizing and Organizing (2004a). Fact sheets: globalization and the informal economy. Available from http://www.wiego.org/,aom/fact3.shtml (accessed 14 December 2004).

______ (2004b). Fact sheets: home-based workers. Available from http://www.wiego.org/main/fact4.shtml (accessed 14 December 2004).

______ (2004c). Fact sheets: women in the informal economy. Available from http://www.wiego.org/main/fact2.shtml (accessed 14 December 2004).

World Bank (1994). *Averting the Old Age Crisis: Policies to Protect the Old and Promote Growth*. Washington, D.C.

________ (1995). *Poverty in Russia: An Assessment*. Report No. 14110-RU. Human Resources Division. Europe and Central Asia Country Department III. Available from http://www-wds.worldbank.org/servlet/WDSContentServer/WDSP/IB/1995/06/13/000009265_3961019104239/Rendered/PDF/multi0page.pdf (accessed 18 April 2005).

______ (1997). *World Development Report, 1997: The State in a Changing World*. New York: Oxford University Press.

_______ (2000). *World Development Report, 2000/2001: Attacking Poverty*. New York: Oxford University Press.

_____ (2004a). *Global Economic Prospects, 2005: Trade, Regionalism and Development*. Washington, D.C., p. 13. November.

______ (2004b). *Inequality in Latin America: Breaking with History?* Washington, D.C.

_______ (2004c). *Social Development in World Bank Operations: Results and Way Forward*. Washington, D.C., p. 17.

_______ (2005). Board presentations of PRSP documents. Available from http://siteresources.worldbank.org/INTPRS1/Resources/boardlist.pdf (accessed 29 April 2005).

World Economic Forum (2004). Voice of the people, 2004: survey on trust, 2004. Available from http://www.weforum.org/site/homepublic.nsf/Content/Surveys%5CVoice+of+the+People+2004 (accessed 21 April 2005).

World Health Organization (2002). *World Report on Violence and Health*. Geneva, p. 89-91 and 100.

______ (2003). *The World Health Report, 2003: Shaping the Future*. Geneva.

______ (2004). *The World Health Report, 2004—HIV/AIDS: Changing History*. Geneva.

______ (2005a). Obesity and overweight. Global Strategy on Diet, Physical Activity and Health. Available from http://www.who.int/dietphysicalactivity/publications/facts/obesity/en/ (accessed 12 April 2005).

______ (2005b). *The World Health Report: Making Every Mother and Child Count*. Geneva.

World Information Transfer (2005). *World Ecology Report*, vol. XVII, No. 1 (spring).

Worldwatch Institute (2003). Severe weather events on the rise. *Vital Signs, 2003*. New York: W.W. Norton and Company.

كيفية الحصول على منشورات الأمم المتحدة

يمكن الحصول على منشورات الأمم المتحدة من المكتبات ودور التوزيع في جميع أنحاء العالم . استعلم عنها من المكتبة التي تتعامل معها أو اكتب إلى : الأمم المتحدة ، قسم البيع في نيويورك أو في جنيف .

如何购取联合国出版物

联合国出版物在全世界各地的书店和经售处均有发售。请向书店询问或写信到纽约或日内瓦的联合国销售组。

HOW TO OBTAIN UNITED NATIONS PUBLICATIONS

United Nations publications may be obtained from bookstores and distributors throughout the world. Consult your bookstore or write to: United Nations, Sales Section, New York or Geneva.

COMMENT SE PROCURER LES PUBLICATIONS DES NATIONS UNIES

Les publications des Nations Unies sont en vente dans les librairies et les agences dépositaires du monde entier. Informez-vous auprès de votre libraire ou adressez-vous à : Nations Unies, Section des ventes, New York ou Genève.

КАК ПОЛУЧИТЬ ИЗДАНИЯ ОРГАНИЗАЦИИ ОБЪЕДИНЕННЫХ НАЦИЙ

Издания Организации Объединенных Наций можно купить в книжных магазинах и агентствах во всех районах мира. Наводите справки об изданиях в вашем книжном магазине или пишите по адресу: Организация Объединенных Наций, Секция по продаже изданий, Нью-Йорк или Женева.

COMO CONSEGUIR PUBLICACIONES DE LAS NACIONES UNIDAS

Las publicaciones de las Naciones Unidas están en venta en librerías y casas distribuidoras en todas partes del mundo. Consulte a su librero o diríjase a: Naciones Unidas, Sección de Ventas, Nueva York o Ginebra.

Litho in United Nations, New York
37966–August 2005–3,675
ISBN 92-1-130243-9

United Nations publication
Sales No. E.05.IV.5
A/60/117/Rev.1
ST/ESA/299